MAKE IT
OWN IT
LOVE IT

The Essential Guide to Sewing, Altering and Customizing

MATT CHAPPLE

Photography by Simon Brown

jacqui small

First published in 2016 by
Jacqui Small LLP
74–77 White Lion Street
London N1 9PF

Publisher: Jacqui Small
Managing Editor: Emma Heyworth-Dunn
Design and Art Direction: Rachel Cross
Editor: Sian Parkhouse
Photographer: Simon Brown
  except for pp32/33 photographer Simon Upton
  and p55 photographer Michael Sinclair
Props and styling: Caroline Davis
Production: Maeve Healy

ISBN: 978 1 84780 894 3

A catalogue record for this book is available
from the British Library.

2018 2017 2016
10 9 8 7 6 5 4 3 2 1

Printed in China

Matt Chapple's creative lifestyle blog sewwhatsnew.co.uk
features stitching and craft ideas for the whole family.

Quarto is the authority on a wide range of topics.

Quarto educates, entertains and enriches the lives of
our readers – enthusiasts and lovers of hands-on living.

www.QuartoKnows.com

CONTENTS

Welcome

Hi. I'm Matt Chapple, and I was the winner of BBC2's *Great British Sewing Bee* in 2015.

It was for this programme that I made and customized 18 garments, ranging from dresses and trousers to a kilt and a leather jacket in just six rigorous weeks, until I was crowned the first ever male champion. My previously secret passion for stitching was now well and truly out!

I joined the army when I was 16, and was trained as a vehicle mechanic. My time in the armed forces taught me many skills, of which sewing and general upkeep of my uniform and kit was one. My passion for sewing actually began, believe it or not, with a curtain. I was surprised at the cost of made-to-measure curtains. So when my wife, Gemma, went out one night I knocked one up. You can imagine the smiles and the raised eyebrows it received.

As my family has grown so has my sewing repertoire, to the stage where I am not just doing running repairs, but actually creating and personalizing items for myself and others to wear with pride. The *Great British Sewing Bee* gave me the confidence to be more experimental with my projects, and I now truly value the freedom that sewing allows me. I begin with a blank canvas and get to choose the type of garment, the fabric and the fit, enabling me to create a truly one-off item.

Make it, Own it, Love it is my debut book and showcases something extremely close to my heart, the fact that we can all create something unique, whether it be from scratch or as part of a customization. High-street shops have given us competitive prices and online shopping access to a huge variety of clothes at the touch of a button. But I want us to still have the confidence to use core skills, such as repairing a pocket or mending a hem, so that we love our clothes and don't just replace them. Or alternatively we can take something mainstream and turn it into something unique and personal.

That's why in this book I take you from the basics of hand stitching to helping you to find your own style and learn how to apply it to lots of different garments. You will discover how to create something unique without the need for a pattern, and the all-important aftercare that makes a garment live longer.

Thanks for joining me. When I am not sewing you can find me sharing my news, makes and inspirations on my blog sewwhatsnew.co.uk

Now, let's explore your wardrobe and see where it takes us . . .

TOOL KIT TO COOL KIT

Some kit is essential, some is only used every now and again.
But if you need to know what the correct name is for that curvy thing
you've seen, then start here.

WHAT DOES WHAT?

There are lots of gadgets designed to make your sewing life easier – perhaps some of them you even already have in your tool kit, but you weren't quite sure of its name or purpose. I've grouped them into general functions to help you decide what's the best one for you. Maybe there are some things here that you've never seen or heard of before.

I'm a sucker for new things as well as the traditional, so the selection of useful gadgets listed in cool kit (page 23) was a must.

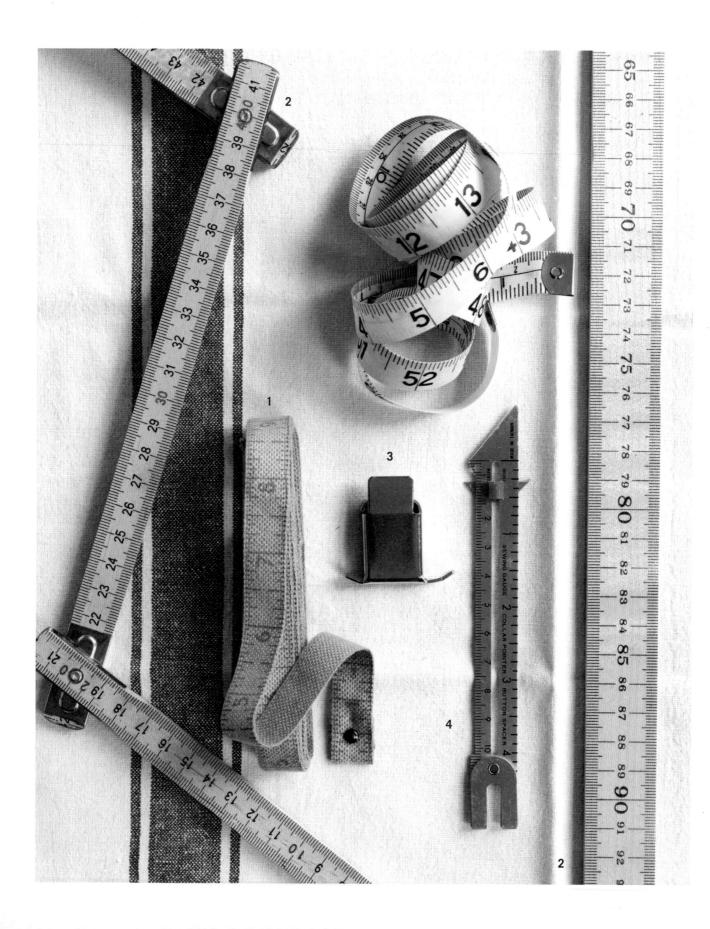

Measure

1. TAPES

Traditionally made of fabric or flexible plastic, but now more commonly constructed from fibreglass to reduce stretching, the tape measure is a staple in any stitcher's kit. Typically these have metric scales on one side and imperial on the other, totalling 150cm (60in) in length.

Tip: Always remember to measure twice and cut once!

2. RULERS

Rulers aren't just for straight lines you know – they come in many shapes and sizes. For example, as well as the straight wooden rule you can get plastic French curve and fashion curve rulers to help mark out the shape of necklines, armholes, sleeve caps and the like.

3. SEAM GUIDES

When stitching or pressing it's really helpful to have a seam guide close by. They are typically metal sliders that allow you to select your desired seam allowance set against a graduated scale and can save you trying to fiddle around with a flexible tape measure for a repeated measurement.

Tip: Join two pencils together with an elastic band, then fold a piece of card and wedge it in between them to give a perfect low-cost seam-allowance guide.

4. GAUGES

A measuring gauge is a light-weight guide to help you with those repeated measurements, such as when placing buttons. They are often graduated with metric on one side and imperial on the other, clearly indicating commonly used measurements.

5. TAILOR'S DUMMY/MANNEQUIN

When making for yourself it's sometimes hard to test the fit of a garment or make adjustments short of having an out-of-body experience! That's when a tailor's dummy can come to your rescue. This will be the most expensive piece of kit, apart from your sewing machine, but is a good investment if you sew a lot. Be sure to choose one sympathetic to your body shape.

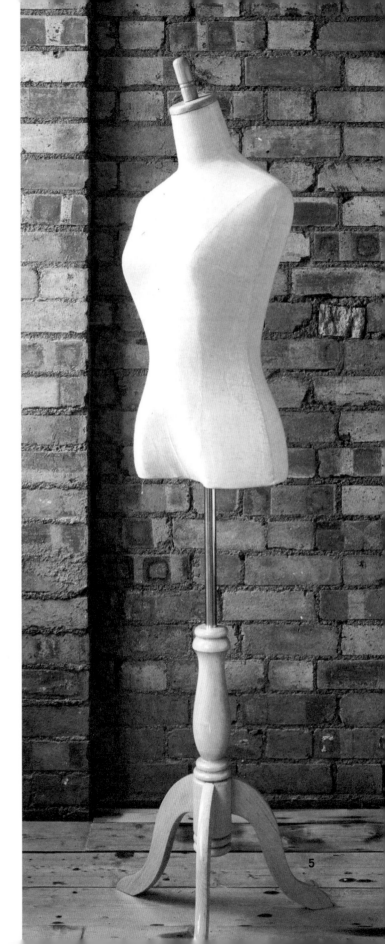

Mark

1. PENCILS

A traditional charcoal pencil can be used to mark fabric, but just be aware that you will still need to wash the fabric to lose the marks completely. Of course for pattern paper this is just the ticket. Don't forget to keep your pencil sharp though.

2. TAILOR'S CHALK

Tailor's chalk tends to come in primary coloured and slightly rounded triangles or squares. These do dull the more they are used, so be sure to trim them with a sharp knife to keep a finely drawn line. These are also available in a pencil and pen form. A light rub with a wet cloth is enough to remove the marked line from your garment.

3. AIR ERASABLE MARKERS

A truly fantastic invention, and depending on the pressure of application and ambient heat, these marks, once made, can last for hours. Be sure to mark and use relatively quickly though to avoid disappointment – there's nothing worse than coming back the next day to see all your marks have disappeared.

4. WHEELS

Spiked tracing wheels can be a great way of transferring markings to fabric, especially if you are copying from an existing garment. Just lay your fabric out and trace your way along the pattern or garment seam line with your wheel, pressing down firmly enough to leave a temporary mark. A light rub to the wrong side is enough to make these disappear.

5. CARBON PAPER

Best used in conjunction with a tracing wheel. Place the carbon paper between the fabric wrong side and the pattern, weighing or pinning in place. Slowly mark along all seam lines and pattern markings.

6. TAILOR'S TACKS

The old-school way of marking fabric is with a tailor's tack. To do this take a threaded needle, and pass it through the pattern and into the underlying fabric, allowing the needle to be drawn through until approximately 5cm (2in) of the thread is left, then snip 5cm (2in) from the other side.

7. ERASERS

Of course a standard eraser is sufficient to get rid of pencil from the pattern paper. However, be sure to use a specialist fabric eraser to remove pencil from fabric so no smudging occurs.

8. PENS

Only use a pen (other than an air erasable one) as a last resort for marking fabric. These can be permanent, or at least very difficult to remove.

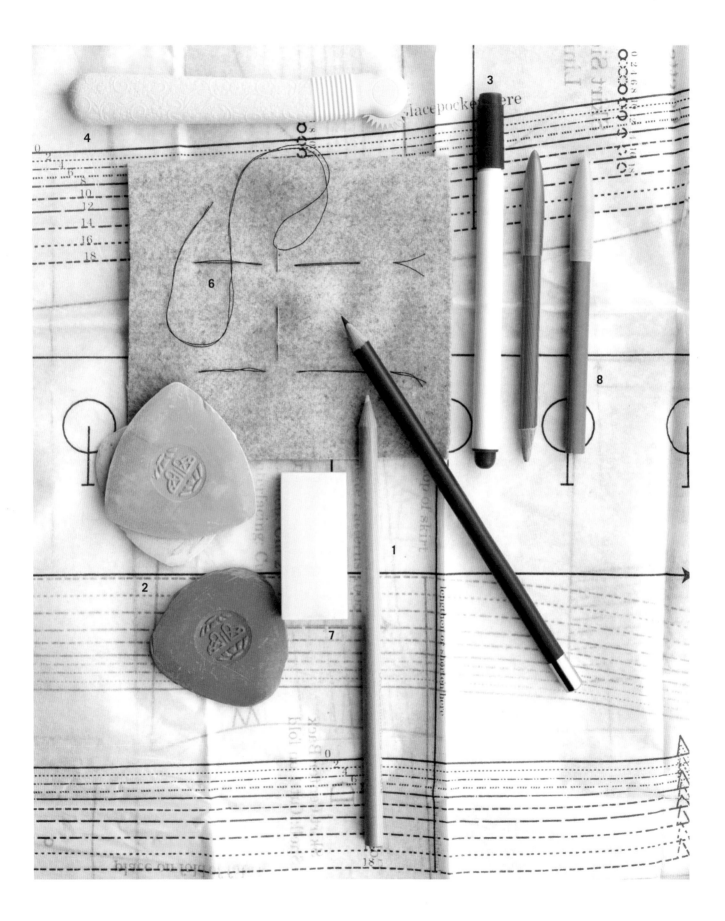

Secure

1. WEIGHTS

My favourite way of holding down a pattern is with weights. They could be anything from large metal washers to mini weights from vintage kitchen scales, but my favourite is smooth pebbles. Just place the pattern on top of the fabric and distribute the weights evenly.

2. CLIPS

If you are stitching leather or a thicker-weight fabric such as a canvas then sometimes bulldog clips can do the job so much better than pins. The beauty is that you can hold the fabric within the seam allowance and don't mark or damage the main garment part.

Tip: They can also come in handy if you want to try on and adjust a garment without getting pricked by pins.

3. PINS

Everyone has pins, but be careful as there are different thicknesses – be sure not to use anything too wide on delicate fabrics such as chiffons or lace. Always try to pin within the seam allowance to avoid marking the garment. Personally, I prefer pearl-headed pins as they are easier to handle and more visible on a garment.

4. GLUE

There's no shame in using glues. Most high-street shirts have a bit of glue in the seams to help during construction. Glues can be a great way to hold a fiddly section in place before stitching. You can choose between soluble and semi-permanent, and some cure even better with heat. Just be sure to read the manufacturer's instructions and apply with care.

5. ZIPS

Zips are no longer to be hidden from sight; in fact sometimes the brighter and more bold the better. You can choose from metal, nylon, concealed, exposed, in every conceivable length, width and colour, even see-through. Zips really could make their own chapter.

6. BUTTONS

A staple that dates back hundreds of years, but oh so personal. Don't settle for understated, why not go bold! Buttons come in every conceivable shape, size and style. If you do want them to blend in you can even cover your own in matching fabric.

7. FUSIBLE FABRIC

Just like glues, this most definitely has its place in today's sewing room. Available by the sheet or roll, it is ironed on in just a few seconds with a medium-heat iron and is fantastic for holding a hem up or securing appliqué so that nothing moves when stitching.

8. PRESS STUDS/POPPERS

Very contemporary in style, press studs are a great way to hold back a lapel, fasten a trouser waist or as a closure for a bag. Heavier ones are formed from a four-piece metal construction, for which you'll need either a special plier-like tool to fit or just a light hammer and flat surface. Lighter-weight ones can be sewn in place.

Cut and stitch

1. SEAM RIPPER
My saviour so many times, this sharp little tool is great to have in case a seam has gone wobbly and you want to have another go. Also great for opening up a machine-stitched buttonhole when used with a pin at either end.

2. SHEARS
A good set of fabric scissors with a long and precise cut is invaluable: precision cutting is the foundation for a good make. Keep them sharp and don't use them for cutting paper, as this only dulls the edge.

3. THREAD CUTTERS
A small, sharp pair of thread snips are great to have nearby when stitching. They are fantastic for notching or clipping into a curve to release the fabric tension. Some are spring loaded to soften the pressure required to grip.

4. PINKING SHEARS
Use these as an alternative to an over-edge stitch to help reduce the fraying of cut fabric. The sturdy blades are opposing zigzags so they can cut through even thick fabric with ease. They also avoid a straight ridge being seen on the right side once the fabric is pressed.

5. ROTARY CUTTERS
As technology has evolved so have the tools. Rotary cutters can assist you in making a precise cut without the need to lift or shift the fabric, enabling an exact cut every time. The blades do dull with use so are interchangeable. They're super sharp so always roll away from the body and keep the guard on when not in use. Rotary cutters should always be used in conjunction with…

6. CUTTING MATS
To help protect your lovely worktop or sewing table from the razor sharp edge of a rotary cutter a cutting mat is a very worthwhile purchase. These come in various sizes and are typically double sided with both metric and imperial graduations and also handy angled guidelines.

7. THREADS
We all know that threads come in different lengths and colours, but it's the quality that's most important when stitching. This is where your money is best spent – cut costs here and you're sure to kick yourself later.

– Cottons are colourful but be aware they have no give
– Polyesters are strong and glide through fabrics easily
– Silk threads should be used for delicate light-weight sewing only

8. NEEDLES
Needle sizes go from very fine to heavy-weight, with their uses ranging from chiffons and silks to leathers and vinyls. The tips of needles are important for each task, with more rounded tips for a stretch fabric, sharp points for cottons and blades for leathers. The numbers on a needle represent the width. The first number is the European diameter in mm, the second is the American size guide, so 60/8 is a 0.6mm or 130/21 is a 13mm.

9. THREADERS
Threading a needle can be a tricky task for those even with good eyesight. There are a few variations on the needle threader, ranging from fine sprung wires that pass through the eye of the needle are threaded and then withdrawn, to ones that collect the thread and feed it through the eye at the press of a lever. Nothing beats a steady hand and eagle eye though.

10. THIMBLES
When hand sewing your fingers can get a good workout. When stitching through thicker fabric or many layers use a thimble, to allow you to focus more pressure on the needle without damaging your finger tip. From metal to ceramic to rubber there's a thimble for us all.

Helpful to have

1. STONES
Used just like pattern weights, a selection of smooth stones are a handy little addition. A scattering of pebbles is lots quicker than pinning a paper pattern to fabric before cutting out. Unlike pins they don't mark the fabric in any way. Next time you're at the beach why not bag yourself some ...

2. BODKIN
A bodkin is a weighty and smooth tool that looks like a fat and blunt needle. It can be attached to thread or elastic to pass through a channel. Great for recovering lost drawstrings and feeding elastics through small openings.

3. TAILOR'S HAM
Ideal for pressing out those hard-to-reach curved seams such as sleeves or shoulders when the garment has shape and an ironing board just won't do. You can make them yourself with a couple of pieces of material and a handful or two of wood shavings.

4. MAGNETIC PINCUSHION
One of the best inventions to grace my sewing table, not only because the magnetic pincushion stops me from sobbing when I knock over a tin of sharp pins on the floor. One wave of this across a surface and they are all sucked back up. But they are equally great for quickly collecting pins as you stitch, with just a little flick in their general direction.

5. IRON
It's always well worth getting a good steam iron and keeping it clean. Nothing helps get a precise finish more than pressing the fabric before stitching or a seam afterwards. The heavier the better when it comes to irons, especially for those times when you shouldn't use steam, such as on wools.

6. CHOPSTICK OR KNITTING NEEDLE
Great for looking authentic when eating sushi, but also fantastic to help point fiddly corners or to turn through narrow stitched sections such as tabs and waist straps. Make sure the thinner end, while pointy, is not overly fine, or else you run the risk of piercing the fabric or the stitching as you apply pressure. A small-gauge knitting needle with a rounded top will also do the trick.

7. HAMMER
Because some times it's not always about the delicate things, and that's why a hammer is a good addition to your kit. Admittedly it only needs to be a light-weight one, but it can come in really useful for compressing those press studs, for example. Also really handy when you are sewing leather and need to flatten a corner or seam.

See illustrations overleaf

Cool kit

8. HERA MARKER
A little known tool but widely used by quilters, these little shaped plastic gadgets are wonderful for marking out a straight line or light curve. Apply a little pressure as you draw them along the fabric and they leave a fine creased line, allowing you to also fold if you wish to. The line disappears the more it is handled so a wash would make it entirely vanish.

9. FABRIC GLUE PEN
Sometimes a glue can replace a stitch completely, and glue pens can allow you to get a precise application without marking the rest of the garment. There are some on the market that will become a permanent fixture when you iron the glued seam, so be sure to read the manufacturer's guidance. But I wouldn't recommend glue for a seam that is load bearing.

10. SEAM ROLLER
A great tool for working with leather, when obviously an iron just won't do. Hold the seam open and press it flat with a weighty hand-held brass roller. These needn't break the bank – you can find them online or from some hardware stores.

11. BIAS BINDING MAKER
There's not much better than finishing a make by edging with a matching bias binding that you've made yourself. These binding makers come in various sizes and are used in conjunction with an iron. You simply draw them along a cut strip of fabric, pressing in small sections as you go and hey presto that's it.

12. BUTTONHOLE GAUGE
Okay so this may be one that you don't use on every make, but when you need to equally space out buttons this is a life saver. You can of course get out your pad, pen and calculator to work out the optimum gap, but this will get it done in a fraction of the time.

13. LOOP TURNER
When you see those sleek silk straps but you have no idea how you'd actually make them. Well this is how. With a loop turner you can sew a thin strip of fabric and turn it through by sliding this long hook inside, catching the furthest end and pulling through on itself.

14. FRENCH CURVE
French curves are a great way of getting a smooth blended line when drafting a pattern. These have great pre-made shapes for waistlines, busts, sleeve caps and armholes. They even have a seam allowance graduation on the curved edge to help you.

15. FLEXIBLE RULERS
These flexible plastic rulers are malleable enough to be turned into almost any shape, but firm enough to keep their form, allowing you to draw super-smooth curves. They give precise measurements down to 1mm on one side and $1/16$in on the other, even on curved edges.

See illustrations overleaf

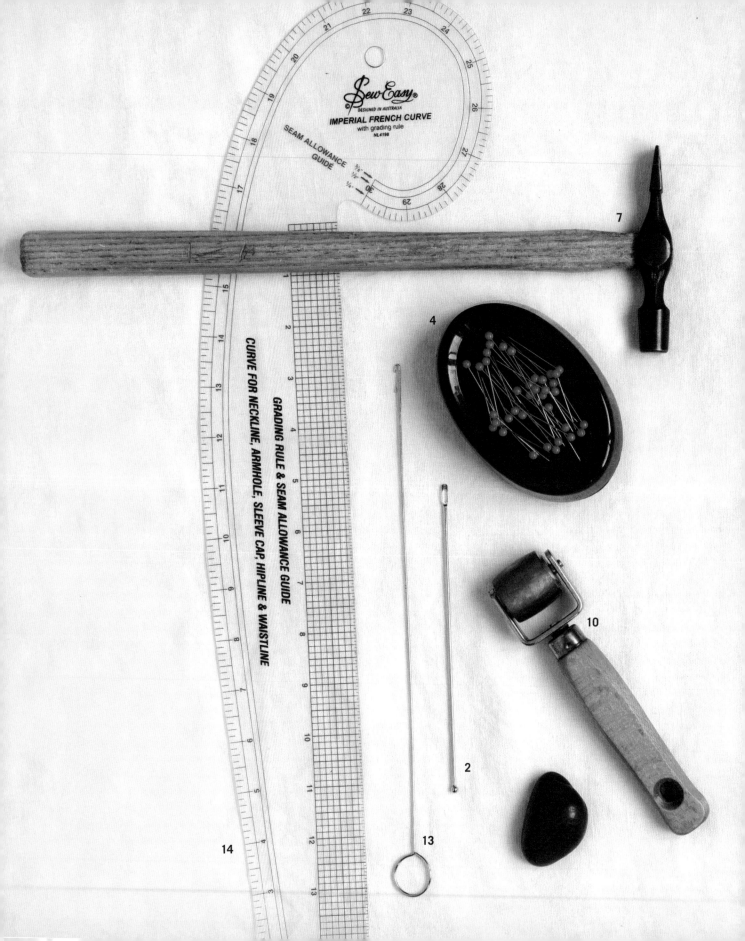

Sew Easy®
DESIGNED IN AUSTRALIA
IMPERIAL FRENCH CURVE
with grading rule
NL4198

SEAM ALLOWANCE
GUIDE

GRADING RULE & SEAM ALLOWANCE GUIDE

CURVE FOR NECKLINE, ARMHOLE, SLEEVE CAP, HIPLINE & WAISTLINE

7

4

10

2

13

14

Sewing is such an important life skill, but unfortunately it's one that many of us were never taught. This book will put that right!

8

11

6

3

2

1

KNOW YOUR MACHINE

When buying a new machine it's easy to be seduced into new gadgets and hundreds of stitch options, so here are my top tips when buying. Price can be an indicator of quality; with a sewing machine you really do get what you pay for. That said, know your budget and work within it. It's all too easy to be tempted to up your price point. Try to see a machine in person. Online purchasing, while useful, doesn't give you that confidence factor, plus there is nothing quite the same as having a test drive. Remember, this machine could be your stitching companion for decades.

At the touch of a button you can have the needle placement, tension, stitch length and width all set for you on a digital machine. It can even tell you which presser foot to use. All of which gives you the freedom to be more adventurous.

Which machine?

ELECTRONIC OR DIGITAL?

Digital models automate many tasks, making your sewing life easier, but the end results are the same as you can produce on a non-computerized machine. So decide which suits you.

1. Spool pin Slide the centre of your chosen thread spool onto this pin. If the pin is horizontal use the spool end cap to stop the reel sliding off. There should be a couple of these supplied with the machine. **2. Bobbin winder** Used for loading a bobbin with thread. Place an empty bobbin on here and wind your thread around the upper thread guide then around the bobbin a few times before either sliding bobbin to the right or pulling out the hand wheel to engage the winder. **3. Hand wheel** Used when manually moving the needle either forward or backward through the selected stitch. This can be useful as your first stitch on a seam to ensure precise needle placement. **4. Stitch selector** Manual machines have one or two dial selectors to change between stitch patterns, digital machines have a keypad. Machines can have many stitches to choose from – refer to the manufacturer's instruction manual for the full range. **5. Power cable/foot pedal** Delivers power to the machine and input from the foot control. **6. On/off switch** Isolates the machine from electrical use. (The hand wheel will still be operational.) **7. Extension table/free arm** The extension table gives more surface area to work on, but also conceals a handy store for bobbins, presser feet, etc. Sliding the extension table off to the left reveals the free arm, used for stitching sleeves and legs. **8. Bobbin casing** Where the wound bobbin is placed. Modern machines tend to be top loaded, allowing you to see when you're running low. Again, refer to your manufacturer's guide for how to correctly load. **9. Feed dog controller** Once the extension table is removed this should reveal the feed dog controller. Moving this lever lowers the feed dogs, which can assist with embroidery, applying buttons, etc. as the fabric is not automatically fed through on each stitch until reset. **10. Presser foot lift** Raises the presser foot to release the pressure on the fabric. These tend to have a second stage of lift to assist with bulky fabrics. **11. Reverse stitch** Use this to place a backstitch on a seam – a great way to secure a row of stitching without needing to tie off loose threads. **12. Thread cutter** There are probably a few of these on your machine, on the left-hand end or behind the needle shaft are the most common places. Saves you needing a pair of thread cutters to hand. **13. Thread Guide** Delivers the thread to the needle. **14. Thread take-up** The internal arm lifts the thread as the needle raises at the end of each stitch. **15. Tension control** A vital part of the machine, this allows you to adjust how the stitch goes through your fabric. Too high and it may pull and pucker the fabric, too low and it may become loose. Most machines have a general/optimal setting shown in bold.

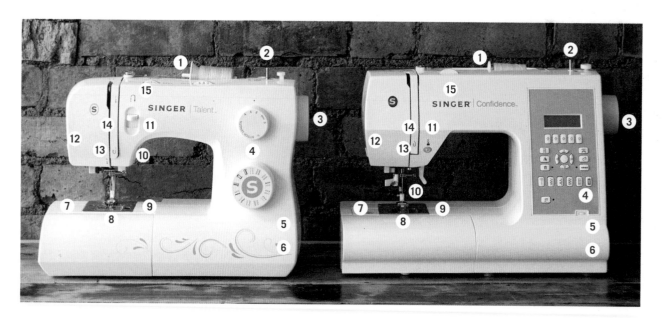

PRESSER FEET

You can do a lot with a sewing machine and a standard presser foot, but you can make life easier, get optimal results and achieve tricky effects with the correct foot.

1. Standard foot Has a long central slot allowing it to be used for the majority of stitches **2. Over-edge foot** The brushes on this foot allow the threads of a zigzag stitch to wrap around the raw edge of the fabric. **3. Edge-stitch foot** The guide in the centre of this foot evenly aligns the raw edge and needle. This foot can also be used to stitch a blind hem. **4. Adjustable blind-hem foot** Blind hemming takes a bit of getting used to. The adjustable part of this foot means you can perfect an almost invisible pin-prick stitch every time. **5. Rolled-hem foot** Rolled hems are tricky to master, but this foot has a curved metal guide that helps to turn the fabric in on itself and deliver it to the needle rolled and ready for stitching. **6. Adjustable bias-binding foot** These feet are a fantastic invention, allowing you to offer up unpinned bias binding and fabric at the same time, letting you focus on an exact stitch. **7. Zipper foot** Used for exposed or standard zips, this foot has a grooved underside, allowing the zipper tape to be guided as you stitch. **8. Concealed zipper foot** Similar to the standard zipper foot, the concealed zipper foot has two grooves, enabling the unfurled teeth to be held away from the needle while stitching. **9. Roller or teflon feet** Primarily used when sewing leather or plastic-coated fabrics. The roller or teflon feet stop the presser foot from sticking and allow the fabric to be released. **10. Walking foot** When stitching thicker fabrics a walking foot helps to 'walk' all layers of the fabric through at the same speed as the feed dogs. This can also be useful for leathers. **11. Buttonhole foot** The adjustable part in the back of this foot holds the button and helps the machine to know when to stop, creating a precise buttonhole for the button.

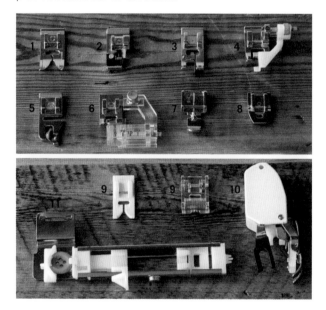

AT THE SHARP END

Already know a thread guide from a feed dog? If not, let me point them out.

1. **Needle plate**
2. **Seam guide**
3. **Feed dogs**
4. **Presser foot**
5. **Presser foot release** *(behind needle)*
6. **Needle**
7. **Needle threader**
8. **Thread guide**
9. **Buttonhole lever**

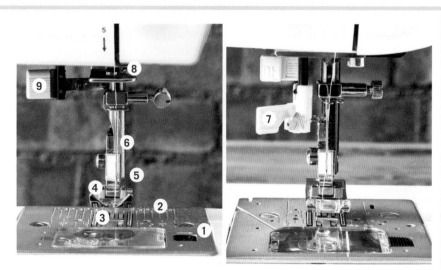

FABRICS

There are plenty of fabrics out there, but what's most important is to match the right fabric for the right job. I'm going to run you through a selection of the different ones that you'll find and a few examples of their uses.

CHOOSING YOUR FABRIC

I believe there is nothing better than making your own garments, but just as important as what you're going to make is what it's going to be made out of. Fabrics are one of the most vital elements to making your item stand out. Let me guide you through the different choices you'll find in most haberdasheries and online. They all have different qualities, so if you're wondering what would work best for that summer blouse or perhaps a stretchy skirt, there's no better place to begin.

Colour and pattern are very much a personal choice, and also depend on who is going to be the lucky recipient of the finished item. But there are some guidelines as to the best type of fabric to use.

Light-weight fabrics

SILK

Famous for being one of the world's most luxurious fabrics, silk has a delicate soft drape with a beautiful lustre and shine to it. This is due to the shape of the many threads per millimetre. In fact, the average silk thread is only 20 μm wide (or 20 millionths of a metre, to you and me). The threads are spun by the dedicated silk worm, which can make an astonishing 15m (16½ yards) of fibre per minute.

Silks are either dyed prior to or following their weaving from a yarn into a fabric. Whichever method is used the most vibrant and beautiful patterns can be printed onto silk.

With their signature elegant drape and softness to the touch, silks are often used for more intimate lingerie and evening dresses, their sheen coming through beautifully in the latter.

Silks can be slippery to work with and will also tend to shift when cutting out, so be sure to weight or pin accordingly and use a fine needle when stitching to avoid damaging the fabric.

SATIN

Man wasn't content at the high cost and intricate science required in the production of silks and so, in order to meet a rising demand for delicate smooth fabrics, set about using technology and machinery to replicate as best they could what the silk worm does naturally. This is when satins came to the masses.

Satins can be found in a fantastic range of colours, but are most commonly seen in haberdasheries as solid block colours rather than patterns.

They can work great as a jacket or skirt lining, injecting a flash of colour to the keen observer. As they aren't very good at conducting electricity they do tend to get a build-up of static. This means they can become clingy when used as the main fabric for a garment.

Like silks, satins can be slippery to work with, but they are less prone to damage. Nonetheless, treat them with care when cutting and stitching.

POLYESTER

As machinery and capability advanced so did the production of quality man-made fibres, with polyester and nylons leading the charge, never more so than in the 1970s.

If you look at the label inside most pretty dresses found on fashion store racks nowadays you will often see polyester or viscose quoted in high percentages. The fantastic thing with these fabrics is that the possibilities of colour and pattern are endless, allowing you to express yourself any way you see fit.

Polyester has many qualities, such as being a highly durable fabric that is incredibly strong. It can hold its form over time and yet can be washed and dried quickly without stretching or shrinking. Be careful when ironing not to apply too much heat as the fibres will be subject to melting together.

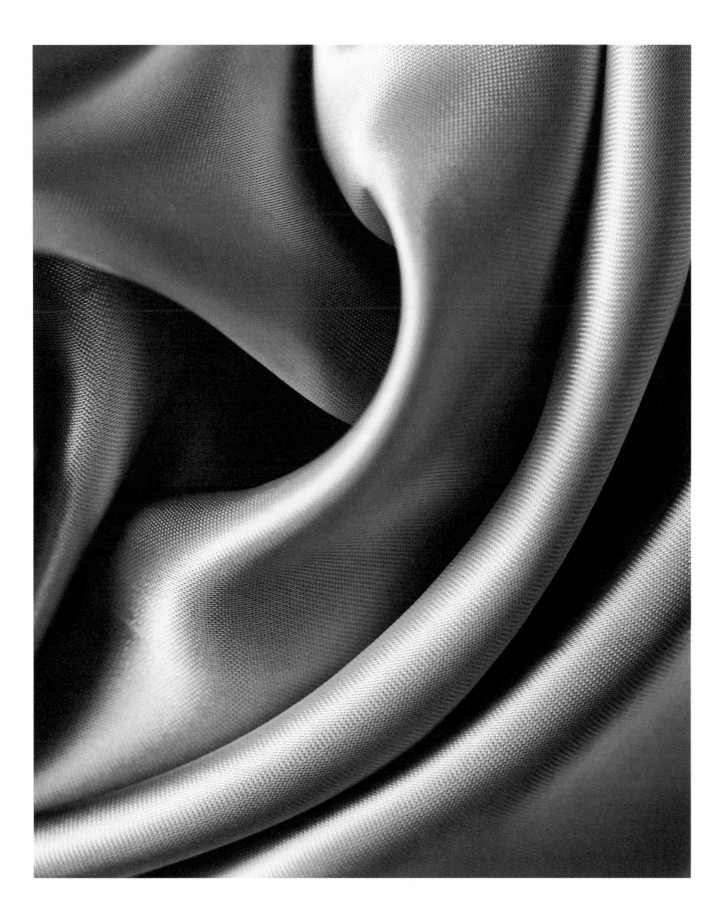

Medium-weight fabrics

COTTONS (LAWN, VOILE)

One of the staples of most haberdasheries and anyone's sewing room is cotton. Originating from the cotton plant, this is decontaminated by hand, spun into fibres and then weaved into fabric. Able to be dyed before or after weaving, cottons are by far the most varied in their colour and printed finish.

Cotton manufacturing is a huge industry and as such costs are relatively low for fabric production, allowing you to really pick and choose your ideal purchase without breaking the bank.

Cottons are very versatile indeed and can be used in a wide variety of garments, quite literally from head to toe. For the novice stitcher a skirt or dress in cotton is a great place to begin, as the fabric can be very forgiving and can handle being stitched a few times before showing damage.

Typically, cottons have a wrong and right side. On patterned cotton it's easily spotted by looking for the bolder printed side. On block colours look for any slightly raised threads or minor imperfections to help identify the wrong from the right.

CHAMBRAY

A type of cotton with a unique construction, and often mistaken for a light-weight denim, chambray is commonly used as shirting fabric. It is made with a coloured yarn running up and down the weave (the warp) and a white yarn going across (the weft), giving a lighter effect that is the same on both sides.

Chambrays can range from light- to heavy-weight. A higher thread count will give the appearance of a thinner more elegant finish, rather than the more durable finish of a denim.

Best used in dresses and shirts, chambray can be extremely forgiving, resulting in a classic look and feel to the finished garment.

LINEN

Often known for its fantastic ability to conduct heat, absorb moisture and remain cool to the touch, linen can be a great fabric to use for summer garments. Ranging widely from tops to coats, shirts to shorts, skirts to trousers, its applications are vast.

It is constructed from flax fibres and results in a strong yet smooth fabric that gets softer the more it is washed. Linen is most commonly found in plain block colours rather than the bolder prints found in more medium-weight cottons.

Don't be put off by the odd knot that can be found in linen fabric – it's not a sign of poor quality. It is after all a naturally occurring product that is not as processed as some others.

JACQUARD

This fabric was named after the inventor of the loom which was used to construct it, Joseph Marie Jacquard. The process of using a flying shuttle to pass through the threads meant that the repetitive process to create a textured pattern in the fabric was sped up dramatically. This led to many intricate designs being developed.

Jacquard has a rich and distinctive feeling of quality and works especially well when incorporated into garments that require a little more structure, such as the bodice of a dress or as part of a jacket.

Heavy-weight fabrics

KNIT/JERSEY

A hugely popular fabric that can be used for multiple makes. The knit or jersey fabric is widely used for dresses because of its elegant drape. It is called after its origins, dating back hundreds of years to the Channel Islands, which became famous for their woollen constructed knits.

Jerseys can range from light-weight single knit, with a flat smooth side and a piled side, through to a much denser and less stretchy double knit.

They can be found in a vast array of colours, and as such jersey is a fantastic fabric for T-shirts, tops, dresses and skirts alike.

Knits can be a little trickier to work with, as the stretch of the fabric tends to make the cut edge roll in on itself – pin frequently to help with this. If an edge has stretched a little when worked, a light steam will help bring it back to shape.

SCUBA (NEOPRENE)

A much more modern fabric with stretch, scuba has had a great uptake in high-street fashion and is surprisingly easy to stitch with. This double-knit fabric has a two-way stretch, which means that it has 'give' in various directions, creating the perfect material to suit a figure-hugging design. Scuba is no longer constrained to wetsuits and can be found holding its own on the catwalk.

This high-tech fabric is made from synthetic fibres – as such they can be dyed and there is no colour loss during washing as with a cotton. It is also quite hard-wearing, so should last well. The construction of scuba can range from a light-weight drape through to a more solid shape-holding weight. If you are ordering online it's better to request a test sample first, to be sure it's what you want.

DENIM

The sturdy twill constructed fabric is known the world over. Renowned for its hard-wearing and long-lasting qualities it has been used to make jeans for over 100 years, in fact ever since the tailor Jacob Davis from Nevada made some reinforced denim pants back in 1873. However, it is the French we have to thank for its original design.

Due to its more heavy-weight construction, denim works best as an outer garment such as a jacket, skirt and, of course, jeans.

WOOL

Warm for the winter and surprisingly cool in the summer, wool is at the heavy-weight end of the fabrics. That said, it drapes well and has a surprising amount of elasticity – this is due to the looser knit used in its manufacture.

While wool can deflect small water droplets it is also very absorbent, so when pressing at home just use a heavy warm iron and no steam. Be aware wool also deteriorates and discolours after extended exposure to sunlight.

Traditional styles such as tweeds and tartans make use of different coloured yarns to give them their distinctive patterns.

Pattern matching

Something that frequently annoys me about shop-bought garments, even mid- to high-end ones, is the complete lack of desire to pattern match the fabric. I understand it takes a little more time and for big businesses that small additional cost per item in the manufacturing process can certainly add up. But luckily as a home stitcher you can really take your time to perfect the pattern match and feel good about the clothes you make. Here are some useful tips to give you a helping hand:

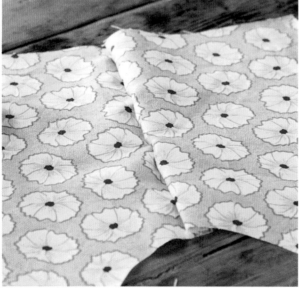

1. You will be using a bit more fabric in order to pattern match, especially if your fabric has a large pattern repeat. Always allow for this when purchasing, measuring and cutting.

2. With the right side facing up, cut out one of the sections that you would like to be pattern matched, using your paper pattern as required.

3. With this cut-out section identify the edge you would like to pattern match and press under the seam allowance to the wrong side, so that you are left with the precise edge you are matching.

4. Back to your original fabric – lay your cut and pressed fabric on top, matching the pattern exactly.

5. Take your opposing paper pattern piece and press back the seam allowance to be matched. Lay this pattern piece so that it butts up against your cut section and weigh down or pin in place.

6. Once you are happy with the placement, remove the first cut section, unfold the paper pattern seam allowance and cut out your second fabric section accordingly.

7. Be sure to stitch on your exact seam allowance as you have measured.

8. Now put any sharp implements away and high five yourself!

STITCHING

There are as many different stitches out there as there are fabric types, but they all have their different merits. Let me guide you through perfecting some of the essentials.

HAND STITCHING

I often do my stitching on a machine – it's easy, quick, convenient and gives me great results every time. But that doesn't mean that you shouldn't know the essentials of hand stitching. After all, there may be a time when you don't have a machine at your convenience. Plus, there's the winding of the bobbin, loading and threading of the machine, and that all takes time, when you could just as easily thread a needle and set to work straight away.

There's a time and a place for the machine, but sometimes the personal touch can give just as great a finish.

Basic stitches

Here are some of the stitches that we'll be using in the Make it your Own and Make it from Scratch sections of the book.

While you're practising mastering these stitches it's best to have a go on an off-cut or scrap piece of fabric. Use a contrasting thread so that you can clearly see where you'd like to improve on your technique. I'll be using a double thread for all of these, apart from the basting stitch.

THREADING A NEEDLE

One daunting thing for those without good close-up vision is threading a needle. We all need to do it though, and while machines have clever gadgets to assist, unfortunately our bodies don't.

– To make this as easy as possible, lightly wet the end of the thread. Next take a pair of sharp thread snips and cut the thread at a 45° angle. Take this cut thread end between the tips of your index finger and thumb with just a millimetre or two (fraction of an inch) of the end exposed between them.

– Take the needle and hold the eye close to the exposed thread end. Roll from the tips of your finger and thumb to the pads of them, feeding a few millimetres (fraction of an inch) of the thread end forward as you do so and through the eye of the needle.

– Once the thread end is through the eye you can draw it through, either tying off near the needle for a single thread or doubling over and knotting together with the other loose end if you'd like a double thread.

RUNNING STITCH

Possibly the easiest of all the stitches, but such an important one. Take a needle with a knotted thread. Decide on where you would like the stitch to begin.

1. If you are joining two parts together, place your fabric sections right side to right side. Starting from the wrong side of one fabric part, push the needle fully through both layers of fabric and draw through until you reach your knot.

2. Move along a few millimetres (fraction of an inch) from where you first stitched and pass the needle fully back through the fabric layers from the other side. Pull the thread through completely, being careful not to pull too tight or it will gather the fabric. You will be back on the side where you started.

3. Again move the needle along just a few millimetres (fraction of an inch) and pass this fully through both pieces of fabric. Draw the thread through until tight.

4. Continue this move-and-stitch motion all the way along your seam.

5. Tie off with a securing stitch and trim away excess thread.

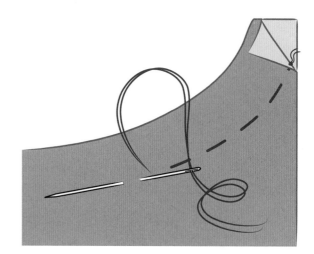

BASTING STITCH

Basting can be used for a few different applications, but primarily for joining two sections of fabric together temporarily while you are constructing other parts of a garment.

However the basting stitch can also be used as tailor's tacks to remind you of specific points, such as pocket corners or zip beginnings and ends, etc. Another key use for basting is to assist when gathering a fabric.

1. The way to make a basting stitch is almost identical to the running stitch, the big difference being you make much longer stitch lengths. This really depends on the distance you are looking to cover, but around 2cm (3/4in) would be fine.

2. How permanent you want your basting stitch to be will determine whether you need a knot or securing stitch. If you don't need it to have any load bearing function or torsion then you can just leave a long thread end rather than tie it off. Be sure to hold both ends if you are gathering though!

BACKSTITCH

The backstitch gets its name because of the motion that you do when stitching; it's much like two steps forward and one step back. It makes for a much stronger seam and is especially good for an area that is going to be under reasonable strain or tension.

1. With fabric parts right sides together, pass the needle through both layers of fabric from the wrong side, drawing through until you reach your knot.

2. Move the needle along a few millimetres (fraction of an inch) and pass fully through both pieces of fabric.

3. Instead of moving forward as you would do with the running stitch, go backwards half of the distance of the previous stitch length and pass the needle fully through the fabric parts.

4. Now go forward a few millimetres (fraction of an inch) again and pass the needle back through, drawing the thread through fully.

5. Continue this two parts forward and one part back motion.

6. Finish with a securing stitch to tie off, and trim away any excess thread.

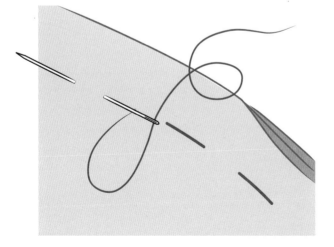

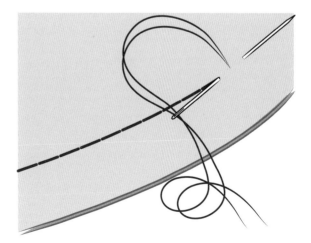

SLIPSTITCH

The slipstitch is a fantastic way to finish a hem. Ideally this would be a double-turned hem to get the full benefit.

1. Working from the wrong side of the fabric, begin with a knotted thread. Pass this through the upper fold in the hem from the inside though to the outside, pulling up as far as your knot.
2. As the needle pops out from the folded hem, catch a few threads of the main garment fabric bringing the needle almost immediately back to the wrong side.
3. Pass the needle into the folded hem and move it along 1.5cm (1/2in) within the fold itself.
4. Bring the needle back through the fold of the hem and pick up a few threads of the outer fabric as you do so, drawing the needle back through to the wrong side.
5. Continue this all the way along your desired hem, finishing with a securing stitch.

BLIND HEM STITCH

Much like the slipstitch, this is another great one for a super-sleek hem that is barely noticeable from the right side.

1. Beginning on the wrong side, with a knotted thread secure the thread to the upper fold of the hem.
2. Move along 7–15mm (1/4-1/2in) and pick up a few threads of the garment outer, bringing the needle back through to the wrong side and drawing the thread through fully.
3. Again move along a further 7–15mm (1/4-1/2in) and pass the needle through the hem upper fold and out the other side. As you do so pick up a few threads of the garment outer, bringing the needle back through to the wrong side.
4. Continue this all the way along the desired hem, placing a securing stitch at the end and trim any excess thread.
5. Don't forget to give this a press as you would have given the hem a good workout.

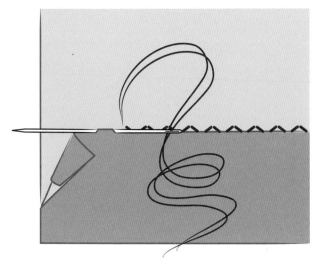

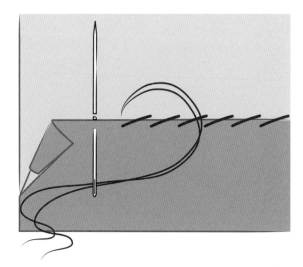

OVER-EDGE/OVER-CAST STITCH

To reduce fraying on a cut edge, over-edge stitch will help to keep any loose fibres in place. This can also be used as a decorative stitch for blanket edges.

1. Begin on the wrong side of the fabric with a knotted thread. Just in from the raw edge of your fabric, pass the needle through the fabric, pulling the thread through to the knot.

2. Loop the needle and thread over the raw edge (this bit gives the stitch its name), move the needle along a short distance from your first stitch and pass back in through the fabric. You'll notice that you're always pushing the needle through from one side and drawing it out from the other side.

3. Make sure you don't pull the thread through too tight otherwise it will pucker the fabric edge. Ideally you want this to lay nice and flat.

4. Again pull the needle through fully, loop over the top and push back in just along from the previous stitch. Be careful not to pass the thread through any of the stitches or the loose thread, as this will cause a knot.

5. Continue this motion all the way along the desired edge. Placing a securing stitch at the end.

SECURING STITCH

The securing stitch is possibly the most important one to get right. You could do a great line of decorative stitching, but if it all comes unravelled shortly afterwards, what is the point? So how do you do a good securing stitch?

1. As you finish your chosen stitch run and you arrive on the wrong side of the fabric, draw the thread through fully.

2. Now pass the needle either through at the point where your last stitch was, or through the threads if for example you've been securing a button. Being sure to stay on the wrong side of the fabric, draw the thread through part way, not fully.

3. Pass the needle through the thread loop that you've just created, draw the thread through fully until tight.

4. Do the same again by stitching once through the threads. Remembering to stay on the wrong side of the fabric, pass the needle through the thread loop and pull tight.

5. Two stitches should do you, but if in doubt add a third.

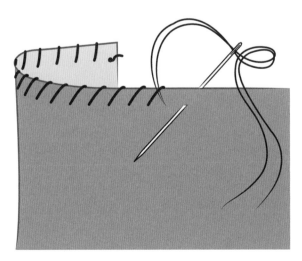

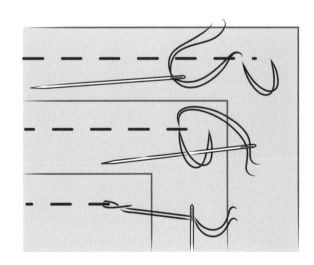

MACHINE STITCHING

While sewing by hand is an essential life-skill, sewing with a machine can make it so much easier and faster. The sewing machine was a revelation when it was made available to the general public back in the mid-1800s, but they have been improved dramatically over the years. Before you start sewing with a machine you need to understand the various stitches it can produce and why and when is the best time to use them, so let's have a look.

With technology there comes short-lived novelty. There are many machines out there with alphabets and a plethora of decorative stitch patterns. Be realistic and think about which stitches you really need.

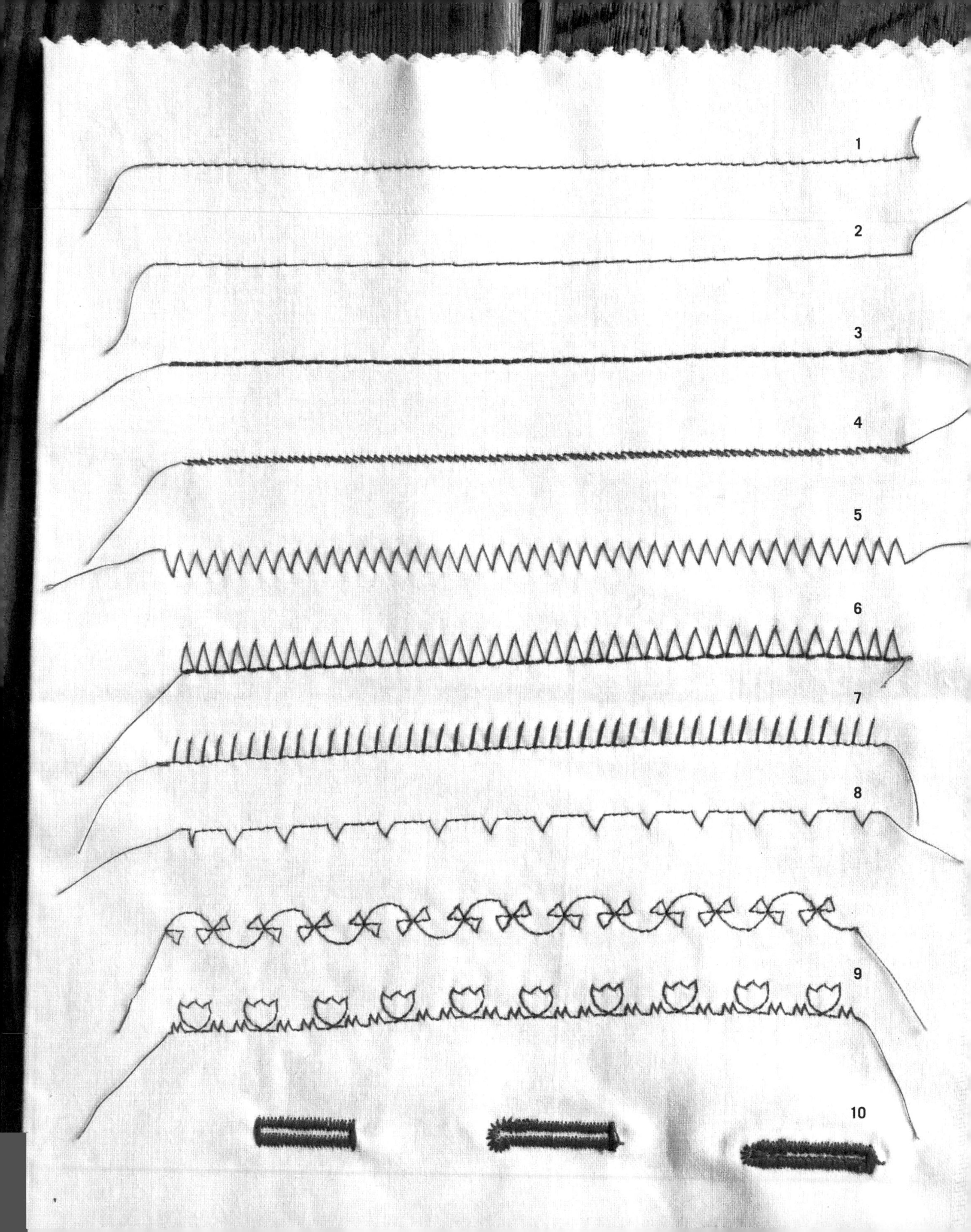

1

2

3

4

5

6

7

8

9

10

Useful stitches

1. STRAIGHT θ-----

The most common of the stitch selections, this gives a simple and effective straight running stitch. Used on almost all seams, this gives a crisp row of stitches to join fabric or pattern parts together.

2. LONG STRAIGHT θ-----

Much the same as the standard straight stitch, but by using your stitch-length selector you can elongate the stitches. This can be particularly useful when basting pattern pieces together or to hold a pleat in place before joining within a seam.

3. TRIPLE STITCH ====

This is a lot like a backstitch in hand sewing. The needle does a procession of forwards and backwards stitching all in one compact row – this results in a very strong yet slender seam. Great for leg and seat seams on trousers.

4. STRETCH STITCH ᴡᴡ

Sometimes you need the stitch line to be close in width but still give an element of stretch to the fabric. That's when you'd use the stretch stitch. If you look closely you will see a row of very fine zigzags.

5. ZIGZAG ∧∧∧

The zigzag, while partially decorative, can be a great way to reduce fraying on a raw edge or seam allowance. You can adjust the stitch length and width to get just the right one for the job. Best used with an over-edge foot, in which case there will be no need to trim down the excess after stitching.

6. OVER-EDGE/OVER-CAST ∧∧∧

A combination stitch using the straight and zigzag all in one. This can be a great time-saving stitch, allowing you to join pattern pieces and neaten the raw edge of the seam allowance in one visit. All you need do is carefully trim away any excess fabric. Despite its name this can still be used with the standard presser foot. One of my firm favourites.

7. BLANKET (ALTERNATIVE OVER-EDGE) /////

Much like the over-edge and used for the same purpose, but instead of incorporating a zigzag this uses a straight and then a slightly angled sideways stitch for a fray-free finish (try saying that quickly 5 times!).

8. BLIND HEM ∧_∧ ᴡᴡ

Used in conjunction with either an edge-stitch foot or an adjustable blind-hem foot, this stitch gives a continuous succession of four straight stitches followed by a left pointing zigzag. It is this last stitch that crosses over to create the pin prick stitch on the outside of the garment.

9. DECORATIVE ⁂ ᨀ

You will find a handful of decorative stitches on manual machines, but this is where the digital machines really come into their own. There's too many to list here, but why not explore and try some out to jazz up a hemline.

10. BUTTONHOLE ▭

All modern machines have a buttonhole option. These can vary between models. Four-step buttonholes mean you have to help the machine, swapping between stages. A one-step buttonhole does it almost unaided. There can be various buttonhole finishing styles to choose from.

I haven't named my machine . . . but we are pretty close! Spend some time with yours, and see what different stitches it can do. I bet you'll be amazed.

A guide to commercial patterns

Patterns are just guiding principles. I like to use them as a starting block for making a garment and then see where my thoughts and inspiration take me.

Another more recent option is the digital pattern. The Colette Sorbetto blouse (pages 126–29) is a great example of a downloadable and PDF-printable pattern. On some websites you can even enter your measurements and download a tailor-made pattern.

HOW TO READ THE MARKINGS

One of the sheets will contain a pictorial guide as how best to cut out the fabric. This relies on two factors: what width of fabric you are using and whether or not you have a distinctive pattern running

through it. The direction of the fabric is important here; this is indicated by a straight double-pointed arrow, and should run parallel to the selvedge (the fabric edges). Try to follow this cutting guide as closely as you can.

There is also likely to be a key with a whole host of terms, some you may be familiar with, some you may not be. I've given an overview in the Glossary (page 172) to help you understand these a little more, without going into too much detail.

The pattern pieces themselves will be printed in clearly marked sections. Also stated will be how many you should cut out, and if you should cut out any interfacing parts to help stabilize the fabric.

A double-pointed arrow with two 90° angles on it indicates a part that is to be cut out on the fold. This means that you will have one continuous piece that is double the size of the paper pattern. Make sure this arrow is lined up along the folded edge of the fabric to keep a precise cut.

Multi-sized patterns need to have a way of distinguishing the different sizes that they are designed for. This is achieved by using differently dashed or dotted lines, or a combination of them. Find the one you need to follow in the sizing guide within the key. Of course, that's not to say you must only follow one. If your upper measurements better suit one size than your lower measurements, then you can always mix and match – just try to blend them sympathetically where they meet.

There are various other markings on your pattern that will be called out in the key, such as notches, darts, pockets, buttonholes, zips. Transfer all marks to the wrong side of your fabric in your preferred method. I like to use tailor's chalk, but it's up to you.

A FEW HELPFUL TIPS

Paper patterns are easily creased, so once you've unfolded and separated them give them a quick iron (warm, with no steam) so they lie flat.

If I know I'd like to keep a pattern whole or maybe use it for more than one person, I use a spiked tracing wheel to copy all the pattern pieces onto dot-and-cross pattern paper. This paper can be purchased at most haberdashers.

When matching seams, pin the notches first and work outwards towards the ends as some easing or stretching of the fabric pieces may be required.

When using print-at-home patterns, one of the pages should have a scale gauge on it. Print this first and make sure that it measures correctly before printing the whole pattern. You can either use glue sticks and overlap the pages or trim back the margins or use sticky tape to join the pieces.

Measuring

When making a garment or altering an existing item of clothing everything starts with a measurement, so it's important to understand the correct positions to measure from. By following this guide you'll be on the right path to quickly gathering accurate vital statistics to put you in the best possible starting position. With sewing I live by the rule 'measure twice, cut once'. If you make an incorrect measurement at the start you unfortunately have the consequences to deal with at the end of the project, which normally is likely to include the use of a seam ripper and repeating several steps, so extra time spent at this stage is well worth it.

If you are making an alteration or garment for someone else, it's very easy to ensure the tape measure is level to gather an accurate reading, but it's trickier to do this on yourself. If you do need to take your own measurements it's always worth asking someone to help. However, if that's not possible use a mirror to help give you better visibility, to ensure the tape is not twisted and is positioned correctly.

To take the most accurate measurements, peel back your clothing to your underwear.

MEASURING THE BODY

NECK: With the head forward measure around the centre of the neck. On males include the Adam's apple too.

CHEST/BUST: Relaxing the arms to the side, measure around the fullest part of the chest/bust.

UNDERBUST: Not a widely used measurement. This is typically just under the bust around the ribcage.

BACK LENGTH: The length from the nape of the neck to the natural waist.

CROWN TO CUFF: With a bend in the arm, measure the length from the end of the shoulder to the wrist.

WAIST: The waistline is the line around the smallest section of the midriff. It's the natural point at which you bend to the side.

HIP/BOTTOM/SEAT: Place the tape around the fullest part of the hips.

RISE: Hold the tape at the centre back of the waist, then bring the tape down and through the legs to the front of the waist.

SLEEVE FROM CENTRE BACK: With a bend in the arm, measure from the centre back, across the shoulder to the wrist.

WAIST TO KNEE: Place the tape at the waist band and measure straight down to the centre of the knee.

INSEAM: The length from the crotch to the bottom of the ankle bone.

OUTSEAM: The length from the waistline to the bottom of the ankle bone.

ANKLE: With the foot flat on the ground measure around the ankle joint.

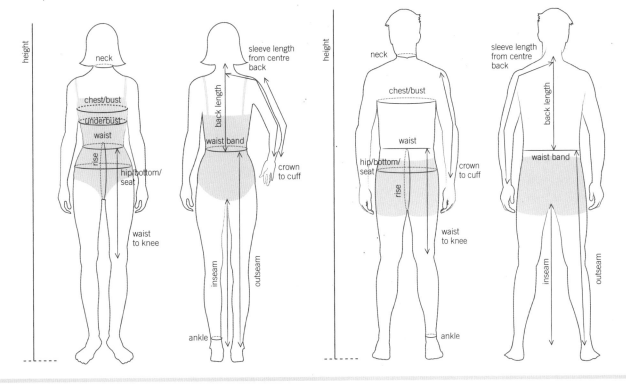

HEMS
Rolled Vs Turned Vs Blind

SEAMS
Straight Vs French Vs Flat-felled

TURNS
Curves Vs Corners

DARTS
Straight Vs Double Points Vs Curved

PLEATS
Knife-edge Vs Boxed

EASING
Easing Vs Gathering

ZIPS
Concealed Vs Exposed

EMBELLISHING
Lace Vs Bias Binding Vs Buttons

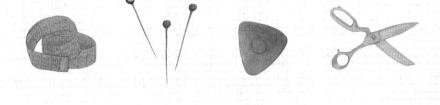

MAKE IT YOUR OWN

In this section I talk you through a few basic dress-making skills, so you can always achieve the perfect fit for your clothes, even on shop-bought items, and personalize your clothes to give them a unique twist.

HEMS

WHY DO WE NEED HEMS YOU ASK? HEMS NOT ONLY KEEP A GARMENT BEAUTIFULLY FINISHED, BUT THEY ALSO HELP GIVE IT A BIT OF STABILITY. IN SOME CASES THEY EVEN ADD SHAPE AND STRUCTURE, AND CAN ALSO HELP WITH THE DRAPE, WHICH IS ANOTHER WAY TO SAY A HEM WILL MAKE THE FINISHED ITEM HANG A LITTLE BETTER.

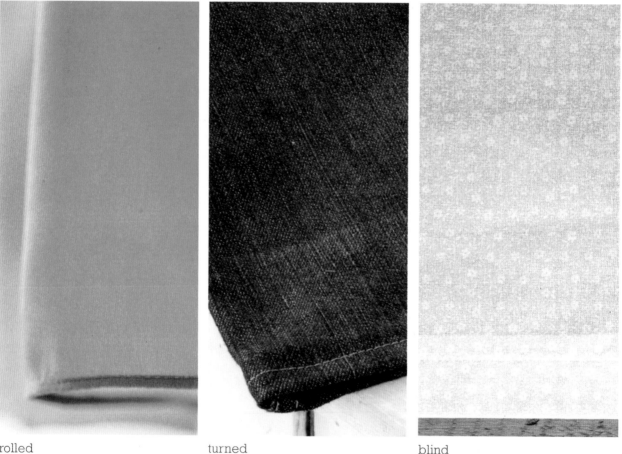

rolled   turned   blind

There are lots of ways to hem garments: single turned, double turned, faced, rolled, taped, blind, serged, to name a few.

THE ROLLED HEM

Which types of hemming style you choose will depend on what you're making and your fabric choice. The rolled hem is typically used on light-weight to medium-weight fabrics and commonly found on garments such as blouses, lingerie or evening gowns. The idea is that the hem is tightly rolled in on itself, giving the bottom edge a bit of weight but not too much depth or bulk, therefore making the item hang smartly without it being too much of a pendulum or a visual distraction on a clean-lined finish.

I demonstrate using a rolled hem to shorten a dress on pages 68–69.

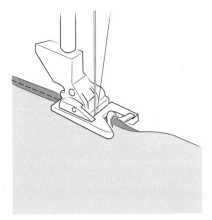

TURNED HEMS

One of the more simple hems is a turned hem, either single or double. Both methods give an effective, quick and versatile finish to a garment and they can be used on most weights of fabric. As these hems are typically visible you could experiment with a contrasting thread – such as the distinctive orange thread commonly used in the construction of jeans – or a different stitch pattern such as a zigzag or decorative stitch. Let's face it, if they're going to be seen why not make a feature of them?

I demonstrate a double-turned hem with a contrasting thread to shorten jeans on pages 62–63 and to turn chinos into shorts on pages 64–65.

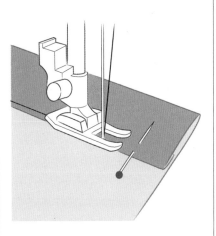

BLIND HEMS

Blind hems can give a really professional, almost invisible, finish to a garment. It's one of my favourite variations, and it can help make your clothes look super sleek. Blind hems are commonly used on dress and suit trouser hems, normally with a medium-weight fabric such as cotton or linen, or heavier weights, such as wool. A blind hem takes a bit more material, so if you want the garment to finish on the knee line, for example, add an extra inch or so to the pattern length to allow for the extra fold.

You can see me use a blind hem to shorten trousers on pages 66–67.

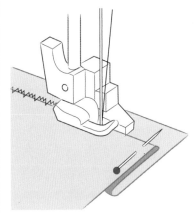

SHORTENING JEANS

double-turned hem

If your inside leg happens to be a perfect measurement for all of your jeans then you can skip over this page. However for the rest of the nation this is a must-read. You can put an end to tucking your jeans up on the inside or leaving them hidden away in a drawer.

During this make you will learn how to measure your hemline, and stitch a double-turned hem.

WHAT YOU'LL NEED

A pair of jeans • Pins • Tailor's chalk • Scissors or rotary cutter and mat • Matching thread • Sewing machine

1. Pop on your jeans. Turn the excess hem on both legs to the inside until the bottom of the new hems are where you desire them to be. Place a few pins around the new hems to secure them in place, then carefully remove the jeans. On a medium to high heat setting, give the hem a good press to hold the new length.

   Tip: It's always good to ask for help at this step to make sure the hem line is balanced and straight. If no one is around use a mirror!

2. Remove the pins and unfold the inward-turned excess. Your pressed hemline should still be clearly visible. Measure and mark a line 3cm (1¼in) below this pressed edge with the chalk, then cut along this new line using either a rotary cutter or scissors.

3. To reduce some bulk in the turned hem, trim down the first 1.5cm (⅝in) of the inner side seam with a sharp pair of scissors, taking care not to cut through all the existing stitches. Fold inwards to the wrong side a 1.5cm (⅝in) hem allowance. Press this edge well.

4. Turn the bottom edge inwards again by 1.5cm (⅝in) to create the second turn. Press the edge well and pin in place.

5. On your sewing machine, slide the extension table off the end and reveal the free arm section. This enables you to easily stitch arm and leg openings on garments (see pages 26–29 Know your Machine).

   If the opening is wide enough, slide your trouser leg onto the free-arm section of your machine, aligning your needle and the inside leg seam. Lower the presser foot into place. If the free arm is too wide for your hem or your machine doesn't have one, don't worry – you can still achieve the same by stitching on the inside of the leg opening.

6. Straight stitch all the way around the new hemline with a 1cm (⅜in) seam allowance. Either backstitch or tie off the thread ends to secure and trim away any excess threads.

Give the jeans one final press and they're ready to wear.

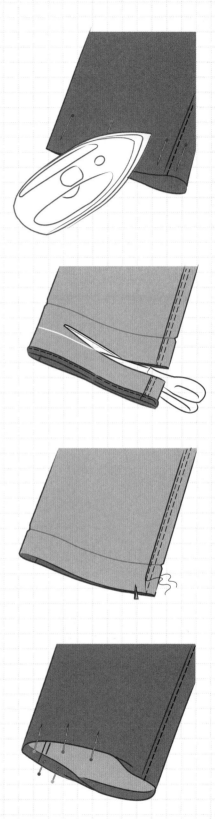

MAKING CHINOS INTO SHORTS

turn-up or standard hem

It's a common problem that trousers fade or tear on the knee. Or perhaps they have a bootcut leg which you don't really wear anymore? Rather than condemning them to the charity pile, why not turn them into a pair of tailored shorts?

Of course, you could just chop the legs off and be done with it. But after a few washes they'll just become a thread-ridden mess. I'm going to talk you through doing it properly. You have two options to follow along the way, either a turn-up hem or a standard hem, so you can choose your finish.

WHAT YOU'LL NEED

Chinos • Tailor's chalk • Sticky tape • Ruler • Scissors or rotary cutter and mat • Pins • Matching thread (or at least not an obvious contrast) • Sewing machine

1. As always, begin with a good press. Then try the shorts on to decide the preferred finished length. Take them off again and lay out on a flat surface, then very lightly mark a dashed line across the legs where you'd like the finished hemline to be.

   Tip: If no one is around to help out I find a little bit of sticky tape and a mirror helps me to get this right – you can re-stick it lots of times to get it spot on along the new hem line you want, without jabbing yourself with pins or making lots of holes.

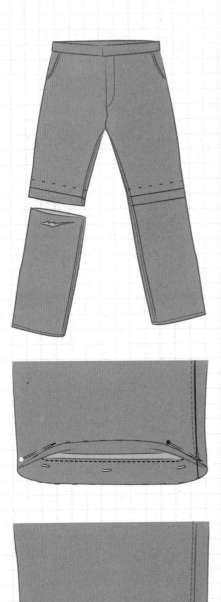

2. **Standard hem:** Mark another line 4.5cm (1¾in) below and parallel to the first on each leg. Do this one as a solid line or in a different colour to help differentiate.

   Turn-up hem: Mark another line 6.5cm (2¾in) below and parallel to the first on each leg. Do this one as a solid line or in a different colour to help differentiate.

   Cut along the second lower line all the way across each leg. If your fabric is a medium- to heavy-weight, reduce the seam bulk by trimming back the 1.5cm (⅝in) of the inside over-locked seam. Be careful not to cut the main line of seam stitching.

3. Fold the cut-off edges inwards 6–8mm (¼–⅜in) and press well. Pin around the pressed edge, taking care to ensure any side seams are laid over to their preferred sides.

4. Now to your sewing machine. Slide the flat bed end off to leave the free arm part exposed. Slide the pinned leg onto it. If your machine doesn't have a free arm, don't panic, just work from the inside of the leg opening. Beginning at the inside leg side seam, stitch around the pressed edge on an allowance of 3mm (⅛in). Secure thread ends by tying off or backstitching at start and end.

   Standard Hem: Turn the hem inwards again by 3cm (1¼in), so that your first dashed line is at the absolute bottom of the hem. Press and then, starting from the inside leg seam, straight stitch with a 2.5cm (1in) allowance all the way around the leg opening, securing thread ends.

   Turn-up hem: Turn the hem inwards again by 3cm (1¼in), then pin along your first dashed line. This should be 2.5cm (1in) from the folded edge. Press and stitch in place along the dashed line all the way around the leg opening, securing thread ends at beginning and end. Finally, turn upwards to the outside 2.5cm (1in) of the leg and press well. Add a hand stitch on the inside and outside leg seams to hold the fold in place.

There you have it, super smart shorts ready for the golf course, the beach or generally any summer day. Well done you – another garment saved and not shelved.

SHORTENING TROUSERS

blind hem

I find that buying the correct length trousers can be quite a challenge. From brand to brand, lengths vary. Also, over time you may prefer shorter slacks for a more modern look rather than a longer relaxed-fitting pair. It's quite an easy task to shorten trousers, which results in daily wear rather than wardrobe wear. You could do them by hand or with a machine, use a single turn, double turn or maybe be a little more adventurous and go for a blind-stitch hem.

 I'm going to take you through the steps to get a great finish with a machine-stitched blind hem.

WHAT YOU'LL NEED

Trousers • Pins or bull-dog clips • Tailor's chalk • Matching thread • Sewing machine • Blind-hem foot

1. Blind hems can feel a little daunting the first time, but rest assured they look really smart when finished. Feel free to try the steps below on an off-cut first to gain your confidence. As for any hem, begin by pressing the lower edge of each trouser leg and a few centimetres (an inch or so) above it too. Try on the trousers and mark the desired length with pins. Remove the trousers and then, with tailor's chalk, mark lightly on the right side of the fabric the new true hem line, then mark equally either side of this however deep you would like the hem to be, in this case 3.5cm (1½in). Ensure that you make your marks equal.

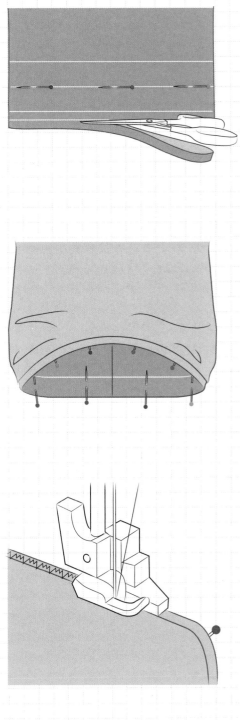

2. This is where that extra bit of fabric comes into play. You should have about 2.5cm (1in) remaining below the lowest of the three lines you've just marked. If you have more just trim away any excess. Fold and press the first 1.5cm (½in) to the wrong side. Fold under to the wrong side again, so that the marked true hem is at the bottom, and lightly press. Clip or pin this in place.

3. This time turn upwards to the right side and line up your two outer marked lines, bearing in mind one of these is hidden in the folds, so you may want to take an educated guess or measure the turned up portion. Pin in place, removing the original pins or clips and press. To hide most of the stitching we're going to work from the wrong side of the garment, so at this point turn the trousers inside out.

4. Now fit your blind-hem foot to your machine and select your stitch. The blind-hem button looks like a rather elaborate zigzag. The width should be as per your manufacturer's guide, but I'd say 3–3.5mm (1/8in) would be good for most machines. Slide the trouser leg onto the free arm of your machine, with the fabric wrong side facing up, and line up the guide in the middle of the presser foot with the second fold/chalk line and lower the presser foot into place. Begin stitching slowly along the hem, making sure at all times the folded edge is butting up against the guide plate. This ensures there are no missed stitches.

   Tip: Some presser feet have a small tab at the front to act as a feed guide. If yours does, tuck the nearest part of the folded fabric back over this, as it will help alignment.

5. Once finished you can turn the hem over and try to spot the tiny little pinprick stitches on the right side. Once washed and pressed your garment will easily challenge store-bought trousers for that professional-looking finish.

SHORTENING A DRESS

rolled hem

Long flowing dresses look amazingly elegant.
However, watching someone picking up the skirt
section for fear of tripping over or getting tangled
up makes me just want to and go over and tell
them (nicely!) that it doesn't have to be that way.

   Far better to pick a length that's perfect for you.
You could of course use a small double-turned
hem, or try a rolled hem. It does require a bit of
perseverance and concentration, but can be well
worth it for a delicate finish.

WHAT YOU'LL NEED
An elegant dress that requires an elegant hemline
• Pins • Tailor's chalk • Ruler • Scissors or rotary cutter
and mat • Matching thread • Sewing machine
• Rolled-hem foot

1. Now is the time to put on the dress. I recommend wearing the shoes that you intend to wear with the dress. Ideally you would have someone to help with the next step, and a mirror also comes in pretty handy. Turn the hem upwards to the inside until you have the desired length. Pin this in place, ensuring an even balance as you work your way around the full circumference.

2. Take the dress off and lay out on a flat surface. If the hemline is not quite balanced, adjust and re-pin the hemline as required. Depending on the fabric type, either use a warm iron to lightly press the new desired hemline or use tailor's chalk to faintly mark it. However, remember that the chalk may be visible until washed off, so mark as lightly as possible. Remove the pins and unfold to the old hem. Measure 6mm (¼in) below the new marked hemline. Cut along this lower measurement.

3. Using your machine, just in from the edge near the side seam sew a couple of stitches leaving long thread ends. This may seem a little odd but this can help a lot with beginning the rolling of the hem. Put the rolled-hem foot on your machine and raise the presser foot up. Place the dress wrong side up, with the side seam about 2.5cm (1in) beyond the presser foot and the hem edge just to the right of the needle. Fold up the hem edge to the wrong side by 6mm (¼in) and feed the raw edge into the jaws of the rolled hem foot. Lower the presser foot down.

4. Reach behind the presser plate and take the long thread ends you previously made in your left hand. Gently pull on them while simultaneously lifting the leading raw edge with a light tension as you begin to stitch. This helps to draw the fabric through and helps the seam to roll. Once you are on your way, you can let go of the thread ends and focus on raising the leading raw edge to keep a small amount of tension to help the roll.

5. As you reach the end of the hem, don't backstitch to secure – just sew to the very end and tie the thread ends off as discreetly as you can. You will have to go back to the first part of the hem and finish it off. Roll this by hand by turning inwards tightly on itself, pin in place and topstitch. For this just use a standard presser foot and try to match the rolled-hem stitch as closely as you can.

And now you have a dress that's the right length, so no more trip hazards.

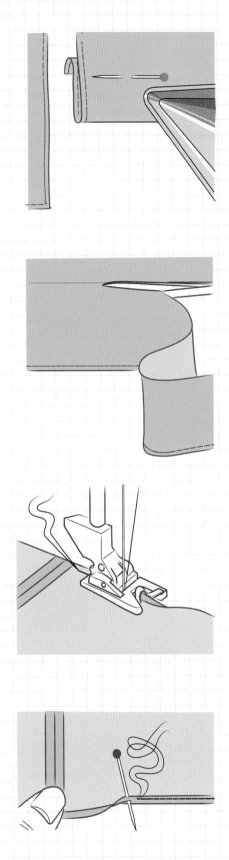

SEAMS

SEAMS ARE A VITAL PART OF GARMENT CONSTRUCTION – WITHOUT THEM WE'D ALL BE SUFFERING WARDROBE MALFUNCTIONS FAR TOO OFTEN. SEAMS ARE THE LINES JOINING VARIOUS PATTERN PIECES TOGETHER OR A SINGLE PIECE TO ITSELF.

straight

French

flat-felled

Here are a few of my favourites types of seams that can give great results for a multiple of uses.

THE STRAIGHT SEAM

Without a doubt the most common of all the seams is a straight seam. It is used on virtually every garment and the one that most of us master first. The straight seam is the simplest way to join two pieces of fabric together. Normally the fabric parts are placed right sides together and are joined along their raw edges. The straight seam can be used on almost any weight of fabric.

To prevent excessive fraying the straight seam can be accompanied by a row of zigzag stitching made within the seam allowance before trimming away any excess fabric. This is also sometimes referred to as neatening the edge.

To further strengthen the seam you can place a second row of stitching either on top of or next to the first row. This can give your garment quite a nice finish when done neatly.

Most of the makes in this book feature at least one straight seam.

THE FRENCH SEAM

Sometimes an elegant garment deserves an elegant seam, something that looks as good on the inside as it does on the outside. This is where the French seam comes into its own. The French seam is one that encapsulates all of the raw edges on the inside, giving strength, durability and a fray-free finish (wow that's tricky to say!). The best fabrics for this are light-weight ones such as silks, satins and polyesters (especially viscose), but the French seam can also be really useful on light to medium cottons too.

To make a French seam you begin by placing the fabric wrong sides together and stitching at less than half of the seam allowance, Trim any excess or loose threads. Turn back on itself, press and stitch on the original seam allowance line. It really is as simple as that.

If you'd like to see me demonstrate it on a garment you can see me use this on the sleeveless blouse on pages 126–29.

THE FLAT-FELLED SEAM

A flat-felled seam is most commonly found on the inside leg of a pair of jeans or trousers, and typically used with denims and also heavier cottons, jacquard, etc.

This is a tough, durable seam that can really stand the test of time and lots of wear. Yet it can actually give a decorative finish, too. Much like the French seam, the flat-felled seam keeps all the raw edges enclosed inside itself to stop any fraying over time.

Unlike the French seam there are three stitch lines in a flat-felled seam: one to join the fabric sections together and two to hold the seam down in place. Typically the outer thread, used for the last two rows of stitching, is normally a tougher, more heavy-weight one, as this has to go through a few layers.

You can find me inserting a flat-felled seam on a pair of trousers on pages 74–77.

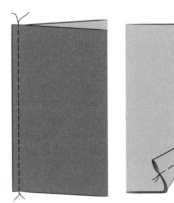
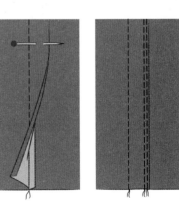

SLIMMING TROUSER LEGS

straight seam

Styles change over the years, but that needn't mean that you need to go and replace your whole wardrobe. We probably all have a pair of trousers on which we like the fit around the waist and hips, but a baggy or flared leg just isn't right and therefore you tend not to wear them as much as you used to. It seems a shame, doesn't it?

I'm going to take you through the steps to slim them down in less time than it'd take you to go to the shops and try on a new pair. This same process could also be used on skirts and dresses.

WHAT YOU'LL NEED

A pair of trousers to alter • Pins or clips • Tailor's chalk • Matching thread • Sewing machine • Standard presser foot • Curved/French ruler (*optional*)

1. As always, press your garment before stitching. Try on the trousers to get a general idea of where you'd like to reduce the width. Turn them inside out and put them on again. Reduce the width by evenly pinning either side of the leg as required. If you have someone to assist you with this step, it helps. Check regularly that you are pinning the same amount on both legs. Once pinned make sure that you can sit down comfortably – it's easier to adjust the fit now rather than later once stitched.

   Tip: Begin at the fullest part of the hip and work down, starting after any pockets. For the inside leg begin no higher than 2cm (1in) below the crotch.

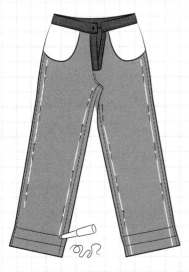

2. Carefully remove the trousers and lay on a flat surface. With tailor's chalk, and a curved ruler if you have one, mark a smooth line where you have pinned (leave the pins in place for now). Carefully unpick your hem, unfold and continue marking the new stitch line all the way to the end of the leg.

3. Load your machine with a matching thread and set to a standard straight stitch. Beginning above your first pin of the outer leg seam, align your garment under the presser foot and lower foot into place. Begin stitching on the original seam. After a centimetre or so make a backstitch and then slowly graduate away from the original stitch line to follow your chalked line. Continue all the way down. Place a backstitch at the end or secure thread ends with a double knot. Do the same for the inside leg seam, ensuring that you come in slowly and smoothly from the original seam. Now do the same for the opposite leg.

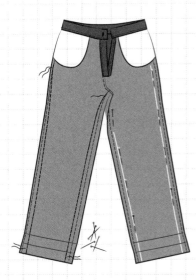

   Tip: You'll probably see that the original seam had a more elaborate stitch over the edge. This is done with an overlocker, and stops the fabric from fraying and adds strength to the leg. We can easily replicate in the following steps.

4. Still using a standard presser foot, select the zigzag or over-edge stitch. Begin slightly outside the start of your straight-stitched seam. I find lining up the straight seam with the left edge of my presser foot is ideal. Stitch all the way along the seam, backstitching at the beginning and end. Do this for all 4 seams.

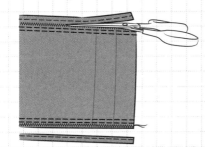

6. Lay on a flat surface, closely to your over-edge stitch trim away the excess fabric making sure not to cut your stitches. Seams should fold to one side or the other. Check at the waistline or crotch of your trousers to see which way yours should go, and press accordingly. Fold up your hemline and stitch back in place. (See Shortening trousers pages 66–67)

SLIMMING A WAISTLINE ON TROUSERS

flat-felled seam

I'm not sure if this has happened to you, but sometimes I buy a pair of trousers and they initially feel like a good fit, only for them to slowly begin to sag a little and become baggy around the bottom. If this sounds familiar, panic not. I can show you how to tailor a pair of trousers to fit perfectly.

The seat of a pair of trousers gets quite a bit of stress – all that bending, sitting and stretching takes their toll. Manufacturers use different stitches to strengthen the seam, from a simple double stitch to a welt seam to a flat fell. The last is my preference.

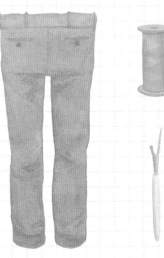

WHAT YOU'LL NEED
Trousers • Tailor's chalk • Matching thread • Seam ripper • Pins • Scissors • Pinking shears • Sewing machine

----

1. Lets begin with our saggy-bottomed trousers. Try them on first and check the fit: decide on how much you want to bring them in by and mark with tailor's chalk. Having someone else to lend a hand pinning or marking can be a great help at this stage as it can be hard to reach around the back and pin them yourself!

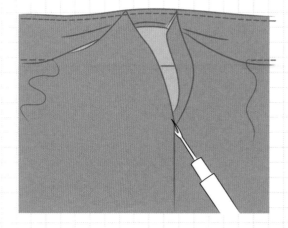

2. Take them off and, using your seam ripper, carefully unpick the stitches joining the waistband to the centre back seam. Work your way outwards from the centre for approximately 5cm (2in) more than the amount you want to bring the waistline in by.

3. Once enough of the waistband is separated from the trousers, you will have access to the centre back seam. Beginning from the top carefully unpick the seam a few stitches at a time. Don't cut the stitches for the last 5cm (2in) of the centre back seam, where it meets the inner leg seams; instead just draw them through to the inside and tie off the ends. Now you should have good access to the waistband. Turn this inside out and pinch the centre back part of the waistband. Pin in place according to how much you want to bring the waist in by. Remember: as you're doing this on a fold, 1cm (³⁄₈in) here results in 2cm (³⁄₄in) overall.

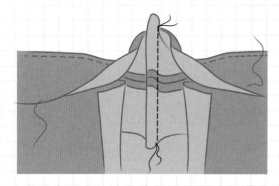

4. Now move to your sewing machine. With a straight stitch in matching thread, sew along your pinned line, removing the pins as you go. Tie off the thread ends and using pinking shears trim away any excess fabric. This will help to reduce the bulk. Turn the waistband through the right way again and give the newly stitched seam a good press to help it lay flat.

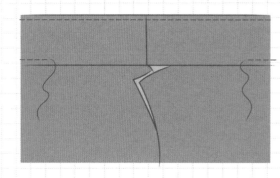

A pair of trousers can get loads of wear, but you don't just have to accept them if they begin to get baggy. Make them fit perfectly again and you'll love wearing them even more.

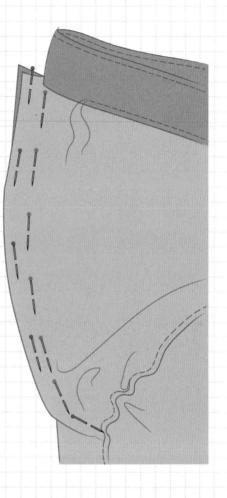

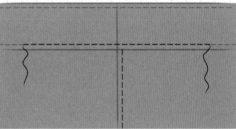

5. Now for the centre back seam. With the fabric parts right sides together pin the two sections together along the original seam line. Place a second row of pins smoothly moving away from the original line until you have reached the desired amount you want the seam drawn in by.

6. On a straight stitch with a matching thread, join your new seam from the crotch up to the centre back waistline, along the second row of pins. Backstitch at the beginning and end to secure the thread ends. Press the newly sewn seam open from both sides.

7. Grade (trim) back one side of the seam allowance to 4mm (1/8in) and the other to 7mm (1/4in). Fold the 7mm (1/4in) seam allowance over the other 4mm (1/8in) and tuck under the excess. Press the folded portion well. Pin the folded seam in place, either from inside or outside of the garment. Place a row of stitching 4mm (1/8in) away from the first seam, running parallel, to secure the fold.

8. Press the new centre back seam well. Align the waistband to the centre back part of the trousers, aligning the original stitch lines: pin this in place.

9. Re-attach the waistband to the trouser by edge stitching along the original seam. Pull the thread ends through to the inside, tie them off and trim any excess thread away.

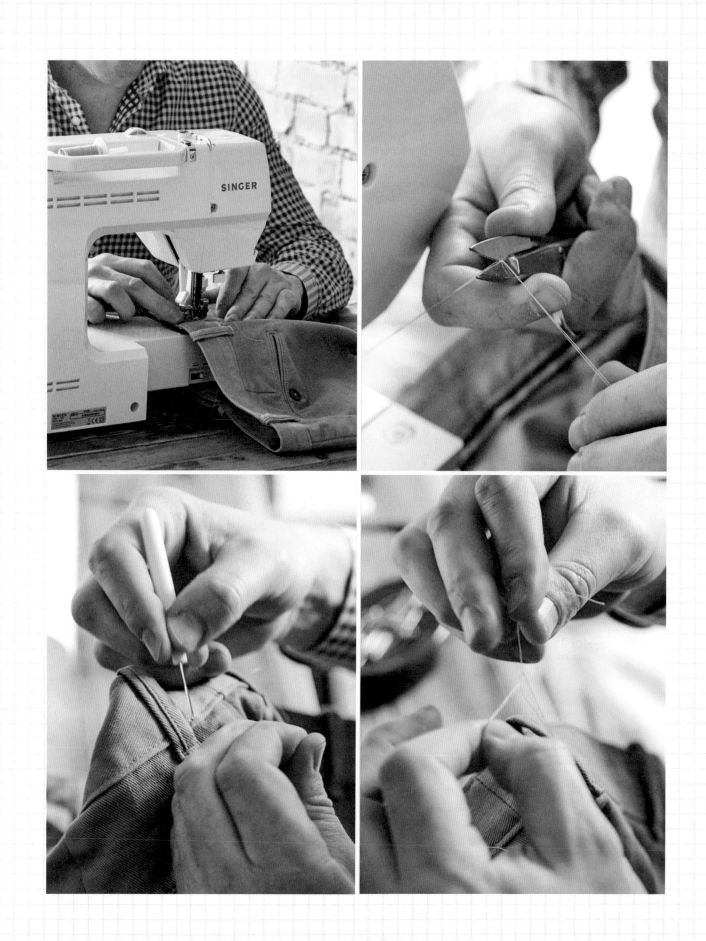

TURNS

ALL GARMENTS ARE MADE UP OF VARIOUS PANELS, THAT'S WHAT GIVES THEM THEIR SHAPE. HOWEVER, RATHER THAN JUST MARRYING TWO PIECES WITH STRAIGHT SEAMS, THERE ARE OTHER WAYS TO JOIN THEM TOGETHER TO GIVE CLOTHES STRUCTURE AND SHAPE – THIS IS WHERE THE CURVED SEAM AND CORNERS COME IN. THESE ARE A LITTLE TRICKIER THAN STRAIGHT SEAMS AND AS SUCH THEY NEED A BIT MORE CARE AND ATTENTION WHEN APPLYING THEM.

Perfecting your turns can be what transforms a home project into a fantastic make, so it's well worth spending time to get them spot on.

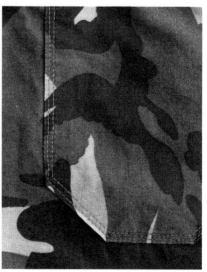

curve

corner

THE CURVE

You'll find that curved seams are an integral part of pretty much any pattern or garment that you make or wear. Whether it is a waistcoat armhole or dress neck edge, you're bound to see a curved seam.

Curved seams are also a great way to add shape and curvature to a garment. For example, they can often be found on a dress that has multiple panels to make up the front and back portions: this allows the garment to fit the figure rather than just hang from the shoulder. Darting can also give this effect (see pages 84–85) .

The main points to bear in mind when stitching a curved seam is to pin often; much more often than when stitching a straight seam. This helps to avoid puckering on either of the pieces of fabric. Once stitched it is important to reduce bulk and allow the seam to lay as flat as possible. This is done by 'clipping the curve', which essentially involves making small cuts into the seam allowance to reduce the bulk or tautness that the sewn curve has created. Make sure you cut close to, but not through, the stitch line.

Curves can be sewn into almost any fabric regardless of weight. However, the thicker the fabric the more clipping you will need for the seam to sit flat.

You can see a curved seam being stitched on pages 80–81, and also as part of the neck edge on the Sleeveless Blouse on pages 126–29.

THE CORNER

Getting corners looking exact and evenly balanced is something many stitchers have toiled over. It is worth taking your time. On a man's shirt or a jacket for instance, you could perhaps get away with a seam or dart being a few millimetres (a fraction of an inch) different from its opposite, but if two collar points do not match exactly it will always be noticeable.

You'll also find corners on the cuff of a jacket sleeve. However, if you look closely you'll notice these are constructed from just one piece of fabric – these are known as mitred corners. This takes a bit more calculation, so if your pattern has these, make sure you understand fully what you need to do before beginning.

The art of a turned corner is to mark the turning point, and to take your time when stitching to ensure a straight approach and exit to the point. You can do this by selecting a shorter stitch length as you are nearing the corner. Trim back the bulk of the fabric on the corner to help with turning through and pushing the point out fully. Finally press well, to get that crisp finish.

As with curves, corners can be sewn into pretty much any fabric of any weight; it's all about what your machine can handle.

You can see a turned corner being stitched on the pockets on pages 82–83, and also as part of the construction of the exposed zips on pages 106–107.

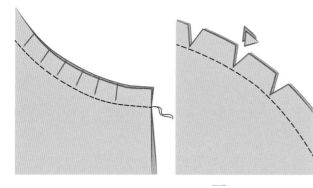

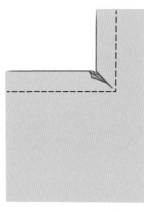
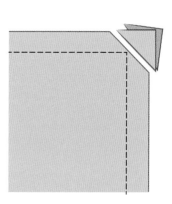

ADDING ELBOW PATCHES

curves

Traditional elbow patches had a practical purpose, mainly to make work clothes last longer under constant wear and tear. Now that we have a larger wardrobe of clothes and our careers are generally less manual, the need for elbow patches has diminished. I understand that, but elbow patches, especially those that are in a bright contrasting colour or a fun shape such as a heart or star, can give a top a completely different look and style. I'm going to demonstrate how to personalize a classic striped jumper using a vibrant cherry-red suedette material, by adding some oval elbow patches.

WHAT YOU'LL NEED
Jumper or long-sleeved top • Fabric for the patches • Pattern paper or plain paper • Iron-on interfacing *(optional)* • Pencil • Scissors• Tailor's chalk • Tape measure • Pins • Matching thread • Sewing machine

1. We begin, as always, with a good press of the jumper and the patch material. Then draft a template for your patch. There is no need to allow for seam allowances; simply create the template to size. To help create a symmetrical shape, fold the paper in half lengthways and then in half widthways. Then you need only worry about drawing a quarter of your shape. Using this template cut 2 identical patches. If you are using a very soft fabric use some light-weight iron-on interfacing on the wrong side to add stability. Cut the interfacing slightly smaller than the patches.

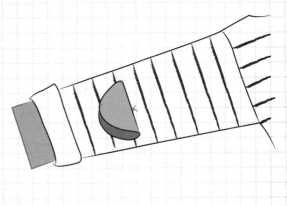

2. Pop your jumper on to mark your preferred elbow patch position. If need be just use a little bit of sticky tape to get a guide position and then use tailor's chalk once you've taken the jumper off. Find your centre point of the elbow patch and place a pin straight through it. Take your patch and gently slide the centre point pin in where your marked elbow point on the jumper is. Angle the patch accordingly. Now pin well all the way around the patch. Keep the sleeve and patch as flat as possible.

   Tip: If you are worried about pinning the sleeve together, slide a strip of card or doubled over paper down the sleeve, this helps separate the layers of the jumper and stop you from pinning the patch and both sides of the sleeve together.

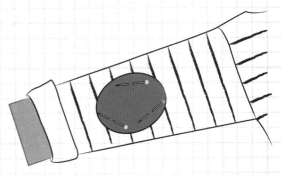

3. On your sewing machine raise the needle to the top and lift the presser foot as high as it will go (most machines have a second stage higher lift if you apply a bit more pressure). Slide half of the garment under the needle so that the neckhole is under the presser foot, now continue to pass the shoulder and upper sleeve section under the presser foot, gathering/bunching the fabric bulk as you go, so that you are left with just the outer of the sleeve and the patch under the needle area. (This enables you to work on the right side of the patch that is pinned to the sleeve.)

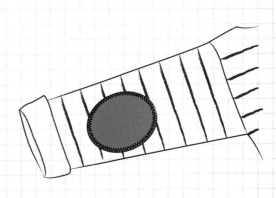

4. With a zigzag stitch, begin at the very top of the patch, and slowly stitch around the perimeter, going just a few stitches at a time. Take out the pins as you go, being careful not to distort or stretch the jumper. As you come back to the top of the patch don't backstitch. Instead finish as close to your first stitch as possible and leave 10cm (4in) thread tails. Carefully pull them through to the wrong side, tie off ends and trim. Do the same to your other sleeve, being conscious to balance the 2 patches.

   Tip: This can feel a bit unnatural at first, but this is one time when slow and steady most definitely wins the race. There's no rush; take your time and the results will be much better.

If you want to include patches on a top you are making from scratch, add them before making the sleeve tube - it's easier to get access that way.

ADDING PATCH POCKETS

corners

Pockets can be a fantastic way to break up a garment and add a bit of individuality or contrast.

The great thing about patch pockets is that you can add them to just about anything you like: jackets, tops, skirts, dresses, trousers, bags. There's also no need to worry about constructing an internal pocket. You'll focus on constructing a pocket, straight and edge stitching, turning a corner really neatly and placement.

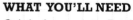

WHAT YOU'LL NEED

Original garment • Patch pocket fabric (ideally the same type as your original garment, e.g. cotton, jersey) • Post-it notes • Pattern paper or plain paper • Pencil • Ruler • Scissors or rotary cutter • Pattern weights • Pins • Matching thread • Sewing machine

1. As always, begin by pressing both the original garment and also the pocket material, as it makes measuring more accurate. Decide on the finished size you'd like your pocket to be. I chose an 11 x 7cm (4.5 x 3in) pocket with 45° angled corners, but you can choose your own pocket size and any rectangular shape to fit your garment: the principle is still the same.

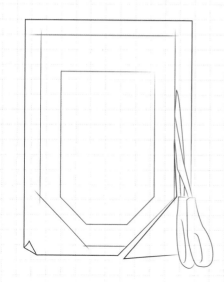

   Tip: Use Post-it notes to experiment with different pocket sizes and positions to help choose the perfect one for your garment.

2. In pencil mark out your preferred finished pocket size on the paper. Once you are happy with the proportions add a 1.5cm (⅝in) seam allowance around all the edges except the top, where you should leave a 2.5cm (1in) allowance. Cut out along the outer line.

3. Lay this onto your pocket fabric and weigh it down in place with pattern weights. Cut around the outside of the pocket. If you are using jersey this has a natural tendency to roll at the edges, due to the elasticity of the fabric. Try not to handle it too much as it will only encourage it.

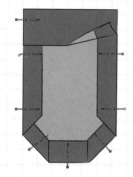

4. Take the fabric to the ironing board, fold inwards to the wrong side the bottom edge by your allowance of 1.5cm (⅝in) and press well. Repeat on:
   – both of the angled edges, being careful not to shift the folded lower edge
   – the side edges
   – and finally the top edge, this time folding down by 2.5cm (1in). Lightly pin the folded edges in place to stop them shifting.

5. With a 1.5cm (⅝in) seam allowance stitch around the side, angle and bottom folds in one continuous stitch. When you reach the corners leave the needle down before raising the presser foot and turning the fabric. This will help you turn a really neat corner. Give the pocket a light press to keep the edge nice and flat.

6. Lay out flat to decide where you'd like the pocket(s) to be, place and pin them to the garment. If you are applying more than one pocket make sure they are placed evenly to give you a balanced look. Beginning at one of the top corners, edge stitch around the pocket, leaving the top un-sewn for the opening. Secure thread ends by tying off or backstitching at the beginning and end.

One final press of the stitched pockets and you're done. Great job!

DARTS

WE'VE SPOKEN ABOUT DIFFERENT WAYS OF JOINING PATTERN PIECES TOGETHER, BUT WHAT ABOUT GIVING THEM A BIT OF SHAPE TOO? ALL GARMENTS NEED SHAPE, ESPECIALLY AS WE'RE NOT THE SAME BUILD AS ONE ANOTHER. WELL, THAT'S WHERE DARTS COME IN. DARTS CAN BE A REALLY EFFECTIVE WAY TO GET A FITTING AND FLOWING CONTOUR WITHOUT HAVING TO ADD PATTERN PIECES. THEY TEND TO BE IN PAIRS AS THIS GIVES A NICELY BALANCED APPEARANCE.

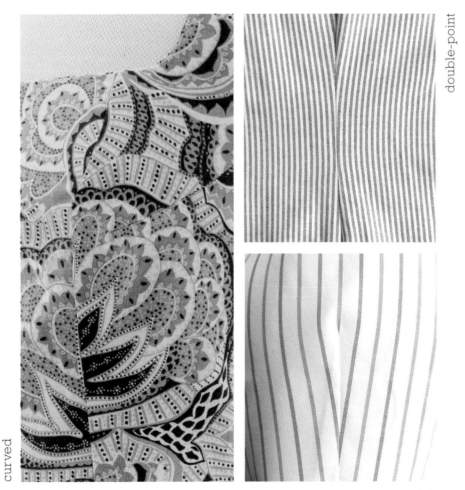

double-point

curved

straight

THE STRAIGHT DART

Possibly the most common of the darts and equally one of the easiest to master. The straight dart is usually indicated by an arrow head mark on a pattern. You will find straight darts used in a variety of places on a garment, but mostly from the side seam just below the armhole, pointing inwards towards the fullest part of the bust, from the front of the hip pointing upwards, again towards the fullest part of the bust, or on the waist pointing straight downwards.

Straight darts can be sewn into any weight of fabric, with the only limit being the thickness your machine can handle. I'd suggest taking care if the fabric is a really light sheer as this will show puckers more easily. If your fabric does need stabilizing, a useful trick is to place tissue paper underneath as you stitch, then tear it away once sewn.

The loose-fitting sleeveless blouse on pages 126–29 incorporates straight darts.

THE DOUBLE-POINT DART

Not as common as the straight dart, but twice as good. The double-point dart is a mirror image of the straight dart projected from its widest point – essentially an elongated diamond.

Double-point darts are often found in pairs and are great for around the bust line or waistline on a dress. Symmetry is key so the finished garment looks balanced and professional. As with all darts, begin stitching at the widest part and work outwards to one of the points, then do the same towards the other point. Make sure your stitch begins at the same mark so it looks continuous from the right side.

You are asking the fabric to change from being straight and flat to being contoured so you have to help it a little on its journey. This is done by cutting into the dart at the widest point (don't cut the stitches!), to allow it to be pressed to one side.

You can see how to construct a double-point dart on pages 86–87.

THE CURVED DART

As with curved seams, curved darts add shape to a garment. They are mostly found on the side of the bust, allowing the fabric to fit the figure.

With a curved dart, instead of sewing one piece of fabric on the fold you cut away the excess in the centre beforehand, so you bring together two raw edges, much the same as with a curved seam.

Sewing a curved dart will take a little longer but will be well worth the time, resulting in an elegant finish. Pin a little more than you would on a straight dart, and as you stitch you will need to ease the fabric a little to avoid puckering – this is best done at a slower speed.

Once stitched make some small snips along the seam allowance. Once pressed to the side this will allow the curve to take advantage of the shape that has been created.

I add a curved dart to improve the fit around the bust on a dress on pages 88–89.

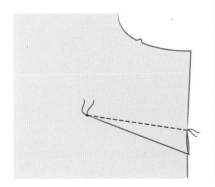

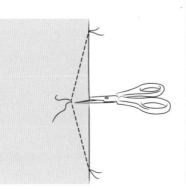

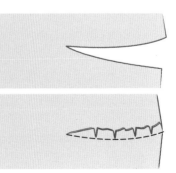

FITTING A SHIRT
double-point dart

Every fashion house has a different approach to fitting and sizing, and it can be common to stick with a brand that you feel comfortable with. It doesn't have to be this way though – you can open your shopping horizons by understanding how you can alter the fit of a garment to suit you.

When I buy shirts I prefer the fitted look, but not all brands offer this. It's therefore pretty standard for me to add a couple of darts to the back of a shirt to create the look that I am after. Darting shirts is also a great option if you have recently lost weight and would like to showcase all your hard work, by creating a slimmer fit.

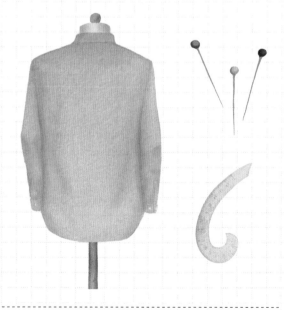

WHAT YOU'LL NEED
Shirt • Pins • French curved or flexible ruler • Tailor's chalk • Matching thread • Scissors • Sewing machine

1. Begin with a pressed regular-fitting shirt. Try it on yourself or the intended recipient and button up fully. Taking a line down from the shoulder blades towards the waistline, where the shirt hangs out from the body, gently pinch the fabric evenly on each side, drawing the shirt in for a slimmer look. When happy with the fit, pin the pinched fabric parts together nearest the torso, and check for balance. Just a general pinch and a few pins are required; the most important pin position is the fullest depth.

2. Take the shirt off and lay it on a flat surface so that the pinned sections are facing uppermost. On just one of the darts, use a tape measure or ruler to measure in from the side seam to the pinned dart, and pick a line that you would like the dart to run on (on me it's a simple straight up and down). Using more pins now, give the dart a more smoothed and even shape by pinning along where you would like the stitching to run. Make a precise mirror image for the other dart. It's important that they are as exact as you can make them.

3. Turn the shirt to the inside. Taking your tailor's chalk, find where the pins join the fabric together: mark the fabric on both sides of each pin. Once both darts are marked, remove the pins and lay the shirt flat. Still working from the inside, use a curved or French ruler to join up the dashed marks and smooth the curves. Again try to balance both of the darts equally. On the wrong side of the fabric, pinch the dart centre along the longest part, bringing the fabric together. Match the chalked lines and pin in place.

4. Using your threaded machine, position the top point of the dart under the presser foot and lower the needle into the fabric. Beginning at the uppermost part of the dart stitch slowly along the marked curve, removing pins as you go. Stitch all the way to the end of the dart. Do NOT backstitch. Once you reach the end of the dart, draw out a reasonable length of thread from the machine and gently tie off the thread ends with a double knot. Pull too hard and you risk puckering the fabric. Trim away the extra thread. Now repeat for the other dart.

From the wrong side of the fabric, press the darts toward the side seams of the garment, turn to the right side and press the stitching line, working out the top and bottom points well.

That's it: a quick and easy customization to make a shirt a bit more you.

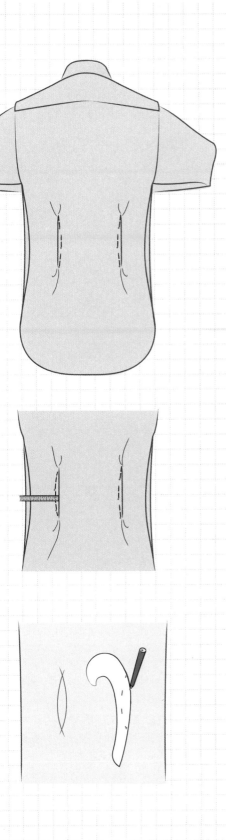

FITTING THE BUST OF A DRESS

curved dart

Just like the chain stores, sewing patterns work to an average size and they can also vary from brand to brand. Even if you have applied your model's precise measurements to a handmade dress or top, there is likely to still be a little room for fitting at the end of the make. This dress is a great example of this challenge: on the final fitting it was gaping a little around the bust line. This is when darts can come to the rescue.

Of course, this same principle can be applied to an off-the-shelf garment. If you find that the dress looks good but the bust could benefit from a little nip and tuck, then this is how you would do it.

WHAT YOU'LL NEED
Dress or top that requires alteration • Pins • Tape measure • Tailor's chalk • Scissors • Matching thread • Sewing machine

1. Start by trying on the dress and doing up any fastenings. It's also a good idea to wear the bra that you are likely to wear with the dress. Once you have located the perfect location for the darts, pinch all layers of the fabric together, with the point narrowing toward the fullest part of the bust. Bust darts should always point toward the fullest part of the bust, narrowing gradually towards a point. When you are happy with the fit, pin in place to secure.

Tip: Try pinching a few different areas around the bust to see what difference it makes. I found that the best area for this dress was on the side, angling downwards slightly from the armhole toward the fullest part of the bust. You may find, for instance, that pinching the centre front works best. The principle for constructing the dart is the same.

2. Turn the dress inside out. Reverse the pinched fabric shape by transferring the pins one at a time from the outside of the garment to the inside. Or you might find it easier to use tailor's chalk or a fabric marker on the inside to indicate where the outer pins were and then re-pin. Once you are happy your pinned line is as you wanted it to be, return to the wrong side.

Optional: If the garment that you are working on has a facing you will need to repeat the pin transfer for the inner facing.

3. Place the pinned dart flat on your threaded machine, positioning the widest part of the dart, which should be nearest the armhole, under the presser foot. Lower the needle down into the fabric. With a straight stitch option selected, stitch from the widest part of the dart in the direction of the pins toward the bust, removing pins as you go. Tie off thread ends and trim away excess thread.

Optional: Now repeat if the garment has an inner facing. Again take the time to pin in place and check for alignment to the outer dart before stitching from the armhole towards the bust. Tie off and trim thread ends.

4. Repeat for the opposite dart. However this time it is key that you replicate the shape, size and direction of the first dart. To ensure symmetry use your tape measure to take key measurements from nearby reference points such as the distance to the side seam, the armhole, the centre front, etc.

5. Give the garment a good pressing after stitching, really working out those points on the darts as best you can for a good finish.

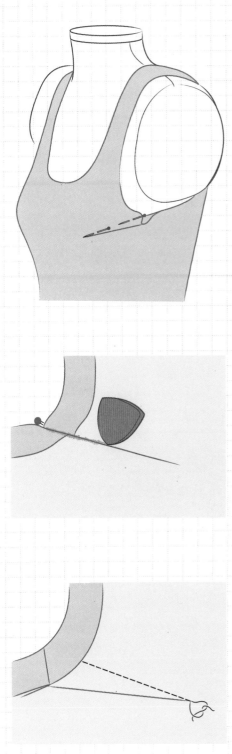

PLEATS

THERE ARE MANY WAYS OF CREATING SHAPE AND DEFINITION TO GARMENTS, AND PLEATS ARE A FANTASTIC AND ELEGANT ADDITION TO WHAT COULD OTHERWISE BE A RATHER PLAIN ITEM. THEY CAN ADD DEPTH AND WEIGHT TO A SOFTER FABRIC, HELPING TO GIVE DRAPE. ADDING A PLEATED SECTION CAN ALSO GIVE ROOM TO A GARMENT WITHOUT MAKING IT LOOK BAGGY.

knife-edge

boxed

THE KNIFE-EDGE PLEAT

Think of the blade of a knife and that's what gives this one its name. The knife-edge pleat should always be well pressed to look super crisp, and if there is more than one they should be equally proportioned. The process is relatively simple and best put into practice on a straight edge rather than around a curve.

Essentially you make a measured fold in the fabric under another fold, allowing the fabric to come back out again in its original direction, stitch in place and press well down the length of the pleat. Knife-edge pleats are best used on a light- to medium-weight fabric such as cotton or viscose, something that will hold a great crease. You can of course pleat wool too, as for kilts, but when pressing be sure to use a heavy iron and no steam.

Pleats do equate to lost space when it comes to fabric usage – if you want a pleat 2.5cm (1in) deep, then you'll need to allow 5cm (2in) extra fabric, 2.5cm (1in) in and 2.5cm (1in) back out again. Imagine you're making a kilt and you have 20 to 30 of these little beauties to make. That's a whole lot of extra cloth, so you can see why some kilts are up to 5m (16ft 5in) in length.

I demonstrate using a knife-edge pleat on pages 92–93.

THE BOXED PLEAT

The boxed pleat can give a fantastic, voluminous and sometimes contrasting effect. Boxed pleats can be used on light- to medium-weight fabrics, however as this type of pleat can get away with not holding a perfect crease it can also be used with more adventurous fabrics, such as scuba, with a bit more spring to them.

The principle is largely the same as the knife edge pleat, except this time you fold under once and back out, then immediately do a mirror image pleat in the other direction. The opposing outer edges should be placed as closely together as you can make them, and then pressed. It can be a little bit trickier to keep these edges butting up against each other when you stitch, as the feed dogs of your machine like to work against your best intentions. To help combat this and keep them in place, it's best to do a line of basting stitch first. Of course, don't forget that opposing 2.5cm (1in) deep pleats actually take 10cm (4in) fabric.

I show how to construct an inner boxed pleat in a contrasting fabric on the skirt on pages 94–97 and a series of box pleats on the scuba skirt on pages 134–37.

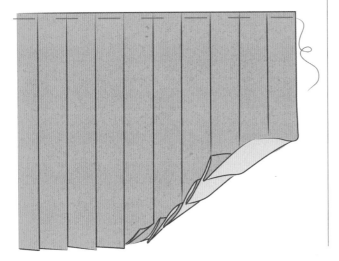

MAKING A T-SHIRT INTO A DRESS

knife-edge pleats

This one is a fun, speedy and really useful remake, and allows you to turn an old T-shirt into a unique dress for a little lady. No pattern is required: instead just use body or finished garment measurements.

The top part is made, rather unsurprisingly, of t-shirting, which is a jersey construct, so this would work well with a fabric such as light-weight jersey or medium-weight cotton for the skirt.

There are options for which stitches you use, dependent on your sewing machine. I used an over-edge stitch, a straight topstitch onto a pleated top edge and a single-turned hem with two rows of stitching to give a pretty finish.

WHAT YOU'LL NEED

T-shirt • Jersey or cotton fabric • Ruler • Tailor's chalk • Scissors or rotary cutter • Matching/contrasting thread • Pins • Sewing machine

1. First things first: give the T-shirt a good press. Measure the line where you would like the top and the skirt parts to meet, and add a seam allowance (I recommend 1.5cm/⅝in). Mark across the full width of the T-shirt with tailor's chalk and cut through both the front and back layers.

2. Measure the width across the front of the T-shirt waist line. Multiply this by 4 and add on a 1.5cm (⅝in) seam allowance at both ends. This will allow for a 2.5cm (1in) deep pleat every 5cm (2in).

   So, T-shirt waistline x 4 + 3cm (1¼in) = width of fabric required.

   Cut a width of fabric according to this measurement. Take the cut fabric, right sides together and match the short edge. Join this edge with a 1.5cm (⅝in) seam allowance. I used an over-edge stitch here, or you can use a straight stitch followed by a zigzag. Trim away any excess fabric from the seam and press to one side.

3. Lay the fabric out flat, right sides together, find the centre of the top edge both front and back and place a pin in. Working outwards from the centre point towards the sides, measure 2.5cm (1in), then mark three points, all 2.5cm (1in) apart from each other. Leave 5cm (2in) clear and then mark a further 3 marks 2.5cm (1in) apart. Continue this until you reach the side. Do this for the opposite side, both front and back.

4. Match the top edge of the skirt part with the lower edge of the top part, right sides together. Working outwards from the centres of both the front and back, pin the skirt and top parts together, folding the pleats inwards by bringing the outer dots of each three to meet. Join the top and skirt parts together on a 1.5cm (⅝in) seam allowance with a stretch stitch. From the inside press this seam upwards. To hold the waistband seam flat, topstitch the seam allowance by using a stretch stitch with a 1.5cm (⅝in) seam allowance. I recommend using a longer stitch length to ensure that the natural stretch of the fabric isn't lost.

5. For the bottom hem line of the skirt part make a single turned hem, 2cm (¾in) deep. Press this upwards to the wrong side. To make this hem line look a little different, make two rows of straight stitching closely together, the first on a 1.5cm (⅝in) allowance. Give the garment a light press, and you're done.

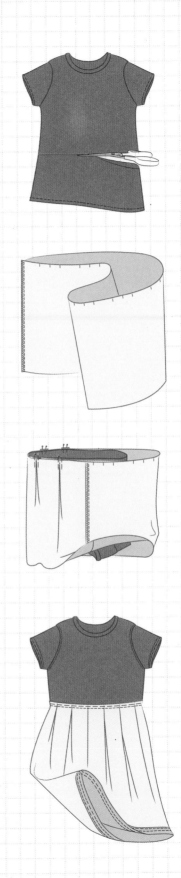

ADDING A BOX PLEAT

boxed pleat

Pleats are a fantastic way to add detail, shape and also create additional space within a garment. And there's nothing stopping you from retrofitting a box pleat into an existing garment. In this make I insert a single box pleat into the back seam of a denim skirt. I chose to do this for two reasons. Firstly, the hem line is fairly restrictive, and by inserting the additional panel it will allow more freedom when walking. Secondly, by choosing a vibrant contrasting material for the inside of the pleat, it creates a unique, personalized style.

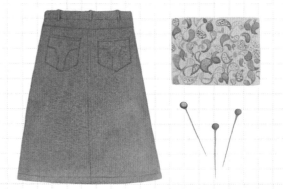

WHAT YOU'LL NEED
Skirt • Pins • Seam ripper • Fabric • Tape measure • Scissors • Matching thread • Sewing machine

1. Begin with a good press of the skirt. Now lay it out flat and decide which seam you would like to insert the pleat into and how far up you would like it to be, placing a pin in as a reminder. Open up the existing hemline and seam by gently easing the seam ripper in to a stitch or two on the wrong side of the fabric, pushing the blade forward and cutting a stitch as you go.

2. Continue this motion up until about 7cm (3in) before your marker pin. For this last section instead of ripping the seam just work the threads out, leaving the long tails in one piece. Once you reach your marker pin, pull both threads through to the inside and tie together to stop the seam from opening up any further. Remove any loose threads from the old seam.

3. The fabric for the inner pleat should be four times the depth of your desired pleat, plus a further allowance for each side seam – I'd recommend a 1.5cm ($^5/_8$in) seam allowance. So, for example, a 12cm (5in) deep pleat either side would result in a total fabric width of 58cm (21¼in). The height should be enough to run from the top of the desired opening down to the unfurled hem. Depending on fabric weight, you may want to press and stitch a hem around the edges to give it a bit of stability against fraying. I'm using a Liberty cotton and chose to hem the edges. Press the whole piece of fabric well.

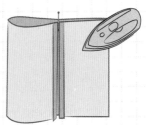

4. Find the centre of your fabric width and mark this with a pin. Do the same for your seam allowances on both the sides. Fold on these marks, press well and then open back out. Bring both of the folded seam allowance edges to meet each other on the centre fold. Press all edges well.

5. Taking your skirt back seam and pressed fabric pleat, place right sides together. matching lower hem and back centre seam raw edges. Pin in place and check before stitching.

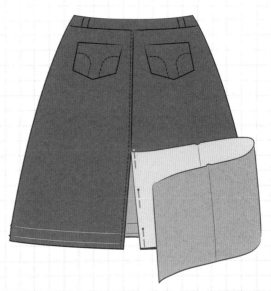

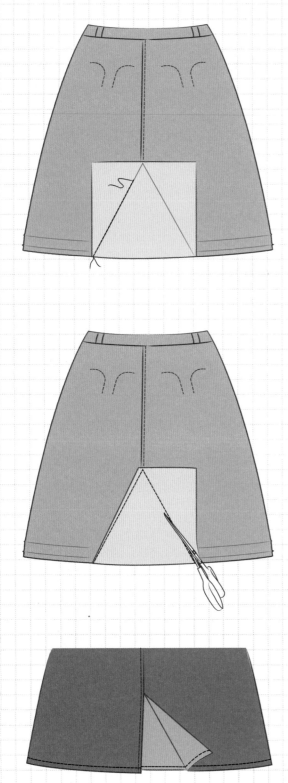

6. If your machine has this stitch option, choose the over-edge stitch. If not, use a straight stitch followed by a zigzag. Join the skirt back seam to your fabric by stitching down the full length of your fabric to the hem edge. Tie off thread ends and press the seam to the inside. Do the same for the opposite side, matching raw edges and hem edge. Again use the over-edge stitch.

7. From the inside, match the sewn edges and balance the fabric pleat insert evenly; this should be on the earlier pressed folds. Draw an angled line from the top centre of the pleat down to where the fold meets the hem edge, pin and sew in place. Do this for both sides.

8. Stitch along the drawn line from hem, up to centre seam, and back down to opposite hem. This will leave a triangle of fabric. Stitch across the top of the triangle if required to bring top edge close to opened skirt seam. To reduce bulk trim away excess from all sewn edges. Fold up and press original hemline of skirt, matching hem depth across pleated insert. Pin in place.

9. Straight stitch the entire back hem in one go, turning as you reach the pleated part, backstitching at start and finish. Lay the pleat flat, matching centre back seam edges. Finally, press well.

What better way to stand out from the crowd than by adding a little splash of vibrant colour to something you already own? But with so many lovely fabrics the choice won't be easy!

EASING

SOME PARTS OF A GARMENT DON'T NATURALLY FIT TOGETHER, AND THEY NEED A BIT OF HELP. THIS IS WHEN THE TERMS EASING OR GATHERING ARE PUT TO USE. SOMETIMES A GATHER CAN BE INTENTIONAL AND A DECORATIVE COMPLEMENT TO A NEW MAKE. THE TECHNIQUES ARE SOMEWHAT DIFFERENT BUT CAN DO MUCH THE SAME JOB – WELL ALMOST.

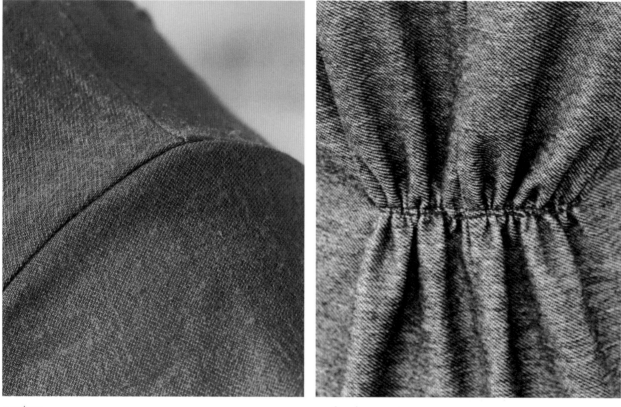

easing   gathering

EASING

Easing is where two pattern pieces are worked independently of each other, giving one a light stretch and the other left to relax so that you create a smooth stitch that allows them to join perfectly without any puckers.

You will more often than not see easing used when a shoulder and a sleeve meet the sleeve cap, typically on a jacket, blouse, shirt, coat and the like. This is done to help the tube-like shape of the sleeve fit into the armhole, and allow the shoulder and arm room to move.

However, this is not the only place that easing is used – in fact it can be found in various places across a garment. From waistbands to centre seams on trousers to curved darts: they all require a bit of gentle persuasion to help them marry up. Most patterns will tell you when to ease the fabric to fit.

I find the best way to ease a seam is to pin the garment as you would like it to fit together, then have the part that requires an element of stretching uppermost. This way when I stitch the feed dogs of the machine are not being worked against and therefore do not harm the fabric. This also allows me to get my fingers around the fabric to gently and evenly help it into shape, while keeping an eye on the seam allowance.

This is not the only way though. You can also ease pieces by taking the longer section of fabric to be joined and make two rows of stitching 3mm (1/8in) apart, one on and one within the seam allowance. Then, while holding both ends of the threads, very gently draw together small amounts of the fabric nearest the raw edge, ensuring the line of stitching furthest from the raw edge is smooth.

Easing can be carried out on any weight of fabric, although it is more suited to something that can take a bit of manipulation such as a cotton, denim or wools.

GATHERING

With gathering we are keen to embrace the ruffling nature as a decorative feature rather than trying to hide it. Gathers can be a pretty addition to a blouse or dress and can give a fullness to something that otherwise would have been more plain.

ORIGINAL FABRIC

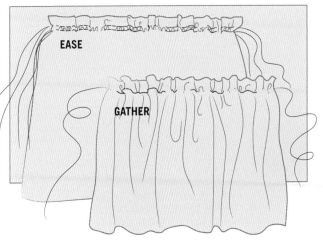

Typically, gathers are found on lighter fabrics such as sheers and cottons. They can look particularly effective on sleeve caps, neck edges and hems, where they allow a little more room in much the same way a pleat does.

There are two ways to gather fabric. The first is with pins, and plenty of them. Pin the beginning and end of the seam in place and also any notches that the pattern says to match. Then sub divide the remaining seam up into sections and pinch or create small folds and pin as you go, always aiming for a consistent balance of gather.

The other is to do much the same as the easing technique but a lot quicker and simpler. This time make only one row of stitching just inside the seam allowance and be a little more willing to gather the fabric into a more ruffled look. You can still do two or three rows of stitching if you like, but one is sufficient. Once gathered, pin this fabric to your opposite pattern piece or into bias binding if you are using that to encapsulate the raw edge and stitch in place.

You can see how a gather is used to improve the fit of a dress on pages 102–103.

GIRL'S DRESS INTO SKIRT MAKEOVER

gathering with elastic

Kids grow up! It's a fact of life. But when our daughter grows out of her favourite dresses I can almost share in her pain of having to pass them on to someone younger than her.

However, as girls' dresses are often made in such a way to hang from the shoulders rather than fit the waist, because they are still growing outwards as well as upwards, there is a sneaky way of prolonging the use of it, or at least part of it, for just a little bit longer – turn it from a dress into a skirt. It's surprisingly easy to do and means that she can enjoy it for another couple of seasons at least.

WHAT YOU'LL NEED
Dress that no longer fits • Scissors • Seam ripper • Pins
• Tape measure • Matching thread• Sewing machine
• 5mm (¹/₄in) wide elastic • Safety pin

1. This is one make that doesn't require a good press first. Either try the dress on your model or lay out flat and decide where the natural waistline should be. Trim back or remove any unneeded extras from the waistline or the upper part of the dress such as appliqué bows. If your dress has a zip in it, this is where you need a seam ripper and a bit of patience. Turn either to the wrong side or in between layers until you can find the stitch line where the dress and the zip are joined (this may be stitched twice to hold the tape flat). Slowly pick away the stitches – slip the seam ripper blade under and cut the stitches on the back of the zipper tape rather than against the fabric. Cut just one at a time until the zip begins to come away from the fabric. Continue up and down the full length of both sides of the zip. Remove any loose cut threads from the opened seam.

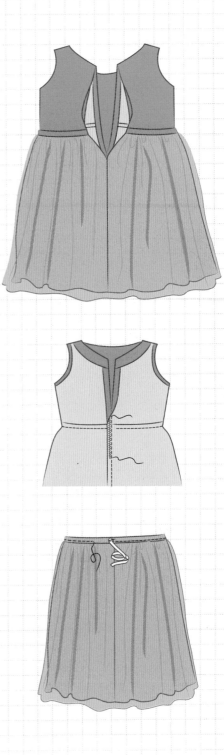

2. Working from the wrong side, lay the dress out flat. Pin the old zip raw edges together 3cm (1¼in) above the waistline. Use your sewing machine, threaded with a matching thread, to close the back seams, including any lining, on a 5mm (¼in) seam allowance. Do this by joining the pinned raw edges from just below the opening and finishing at your uppermost pin. Tie off thread ends to secure. If your machine allows use an over-edge stitch, or if not a straight stitch followed by a zigzag in the seam allowance will help to reduce fraying. Turn to the right side and lay the dress out flat, feeling to match the waistline of the front and back parts. Mark a line across the top part approximately 5cm (2in) above the waistline.

3. Okay now for the brave bit: cut across this marked line through all layers. Turn the upper most raw edge to the inside by 2.5cm (1in), and then again by another 2.5cm (1in), enclosing the raw edge in the process. Pin in place all the way around. Topstitch around the waistband from centre back seam 1.5cm (⅝in) down from the top edge, leaving the last 5cm (2in) unsewn. Remove the pins as you go. Tie off thread ends to secure. This creates a channel for us to insert the elastic into.

4. Take your length of elastic and insert the safety pin through one end. Feed this end into the unsewn opening of the waistband, working the safety pin and elastic around the inside of the channel. Once you reach the other end of the opening, pull the elastic through. Pin one end of the elastic into the waistband and secure by topstitching in place. Pull the other unstitched end of the elastic: this will gather the waistband. Fit as required, pin in place and secure with a topstitch. Close the waistband opening by continuing the topstitch from where you left off.

Reattach any bows or appliqué as desired. Result: one skirt, allowing another couple of seasons' wear and a prolonged smile.

GATHERING A TUNIC DRESS

gathering

A tunic dress delivers well on comfort but doesn't score so highly on creating a flattering look. I'm a firm believer that curves are there to be shown and not hidden so I'm going to show how you can create a more fitted look on a straight-cut dress.

To achieve this, I'm going to gather the back section of the dress along the waistline. The simple action of drawing in excess fabric will create a much more fitted look around the torso. This is also a great trick if you are working hard to lose weight and you want to get a little more wear out of your clothes, before launching your new slimmer style.

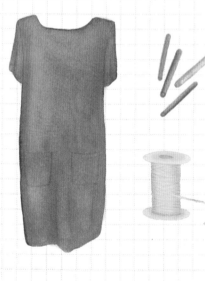

WHAT YOU'LL NEED
Tunic dress • Tailor's mannequin • Pins • Tailor's chalk
• Ruler • Matching thread • Scissors • Sewing machine
• 5mm (¹⁄₄in) wide elastic

1. We start with a pressed tunic dress. If you have access to a tailor's mannequin this can really help with the next step; failing that ask someone to assist. Pop the dress on either yourself or the mannequin, and find the natural waistline. Place a pin in horizontally to mark it. Gather the back as much as you'd like the dress to be slimmed by and pin in place near the torso. Do this in the same way as you would if you were creating back darts in a shirt (see pages 86–87), by just pinching the back in two equal amounts a third of the way in from each of the side seams. Secure each pinch in place with a pin.

2. Take the dress off, turn through to the wrong side and lay out on a flat surface with the back part facing up. With your tailor's chalk and a ruler, mark where the horizontal waistline pin is. Vertically mark the fabric just either side of where the gathering pins are placed. This way when the pins are removed you will have four marks showing you where your fullest width and your gathered width measurements are. Remove the pins and extend the chalk marks. Ensure that the waistline mark is horizontal. Make a note of the gathered measurement.

3. We're going to put in some gathering stitches now. To do this with a machine select the longest stitch possible. Still working from the wrong side, sew a row of straight stitches along the marked horizontal chalk line, beginning and finishing at the outer full width vertical marks. Make sure you leave long thread ends of at least 5cm (2in). Do NOT tie or backstitch. Sew a further 2 rows of straight stitches, each 5mm (¼in) either side of the first row, so that you have 3 even rows.

4. Holding the thread ends, gently and evenly gather the fabric towards the centre, until your outer marks match your gathered measurement. Now you have a choice: you can either stitch this in place to hold a firm and permanent gather, or you can add a strip of elastic to allow the gather to have a bit of bounce.

5. Take a strip of elastic just a little longer than the gathered measurement. Fold under a small amount of each end and pin in place along the gathered centre waistline.

With elastic: Select a stretch stitch option on your machine. Using a matching thread, stitch along the elastic joining it to the gathered fabric. Tie off and trim thread ends.

Without elastic: If you choose to stitch the gather in place without elastic you can just select a straight stitch and place a row or two across the gather. Tie off and trim thread ends.

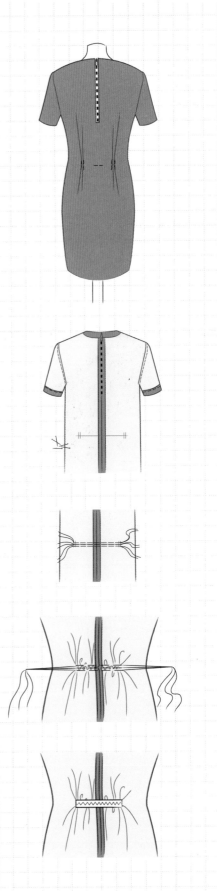

ZIPS

ZIPS ARE A GREAT INVENTION. IN 1917, GIDEON SUNDBACK RECEIVED THE PATENT FOR HIS 'SEPARABLE FASTENER' WHICH IS WHAT WE NOW CONSIDER TO BE THE MODERN-STYLE ZIP, GIVEN THE NAME BECAUSE OF THE SOUND IT MAKES WHEN FASTENING. THIS GAVE THE OPTION TO CLOTHING MANUFACTURERS TO CREATE SLEEKER AND MORE CLOSELY FITTING GARMENTS, WITHOUT THE NEED FOR ENDLESS BUTTONS.

concealed   exposed

Zips can be placed into pretty much any weight of fabric, ranging from light sheers (although it's a good idea to use a stabilizer to support them), through to heavy-weight woollens.

CONCEALED

After making a beautifully sleek garment it seems like such a shame to bulk it out with buttons or a large zip. The concealed zip is a fantastic way to make an elegant closure that is hidden from obvious view and that enhances the overall professional look of the garment.

Concealed zips are usually placed into either the centre back or a side seam. They are stitched to the wrong side of the fabric and the teeth are also turned to the inside, so all that is left is a beautiful clean line.

Here are a few tips to get a perfect concealed zip. As mentioned the teeth of a concealed zip roll to the inside. To get the stitch as close as possible to the edge, press the zip first, using only a warm iron. Don't touch the teeth with the iron as you don't want to damage them.

If you are sewing into a light-weight fabric, using stabilizer such as a fusible interfacing will give a little more stability and reduce puckering.

Always use a concealed-zipper foot for your machine. These are specialist feet that enable the unfurled zipper tape to be held open while being worked on, enabling you to stitch as close as possible to the teeth.

You can see me inserting a concealed zip into the side seam of a dress on pages 150–53.

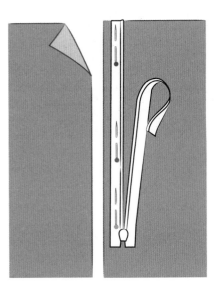

EXPOSED

What was once a functional fastening, hidden from sight, has now been incorporated into designs as a feature. An exposed zip can be a great addition to a garment. Make every effort to use your very best stitching, as it will be forever on show and something that you will be drawing attention to, so you want it to look great.

When applying an exposed zip you have a couple of options. You can either insert it into a seam or apply it directly to the outer right side of the fabric. Either way, due to additional weight that an exposed zip gives, it's advised that you add a stabilizer to the wrong side of the fabric, either a fabric facing or a fusible interfacing.

If inserting into a seam, take time to get the stitch line balanced and equal for both sides of the zipper tape; this will be key to getting the zip looking really professional. Basting it in place first can be a really useful step here.

The good thing about exposed zips is that because there is more tape to work with, you don't always require a zipper foot on your machine. You can use a standard foot and align the needle either left or right to suit.

You can see me insert exposed zips as a feature on a skirt on pages 106–107.

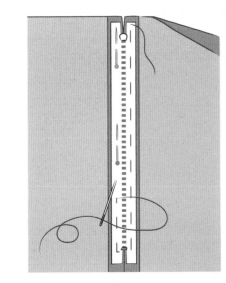

INSERTING AN EXPOSED ZIP

exposed zip

There's a plain skirt, dress or T-shirt sitting in your chest of drawers just begging to be customized, I'm sure of it. The thing is, sometimes we're a little uninspired by the clothes we have, but there's no need to be. Just consider them to be a blank canvas and yourself as the artist. You can do whatever you like with them.

I'm going to take you through how to insert a couple of zipped pockets into an existing garment to give it a whole new identity. If you like, you could always use a contrasting fabric for the innermost part of the pocket to give a little glimpse of something different when the pocket is open.

WHAT YOU'LL NEED
Basic skirt (or any other garment you want to personalize)
• Exposed zip: personally I like the look of brass zips
Fabric for the pocket • Iron-on interfacing (light- to medium-weight) • Tailor's chalk or fabric marker • Pins
• Matching thread • Scissors • Sewing machine

---

1. Begin by pressing the skirt to get a really good starting base. To get your pocket size, take the length of your zip and add 3.5cm (1½in) to each end. Decide how deep you'd like your pocket to be, and add 4.5cm (1¾in). With these measurements, cut out 4 sections of fabric for the pockets and 4 interfacing panels. (If your fabric has some structure to it then you may choose to add interfacing to just one side of the pocket. In which case only cut out 2 panels of interfacing.) With your iron on a silk setting, apply the shiny side of the interfacing to the wrong side of your pocket piece, and press in place for 8–10 seconds. Repeat this for all of your pocket pieces.

2. To mark out the letter box that the zip will sit within:
   – Begin by marking out a line 2.5cm (1in) down from the top edge of your pocket piece. Measure the width of your zip, and make a line parallel to your first, three-quarters of the width.
   – Mark a line centrally between these two.
   – Measure the length of your zip and mark out where you'd like the opening to begin and end – 1cm (³⁄₈in) either end will work.
   – At a 45° angle, draw a line inward from the corner to the centre line. Repeat this from all 4 corners.

3. Pin the right side of one of the pocket pieces to the right side of the garment where you would like the pocket to be. Using a matching thread, straight stitch around the marked-out pocket opening, backstitching at beginning and end. Carefully cut along your marked central line from where the angled lines meet. Cut the angled lines up to the corners, taking care not to cut the stitches.

4. Turn the pocket through the opening that you've just cut. Work out the seams that you've just stitched by rolling them in between your forefinger and thumb. Press the pocket opening flat.

5. Place the zip into the opening and pin in place, being careful not to distort the opening. Edge stitch as closely as possible to the opening. Keep the needle down at the corner, and lift the presser foot to pivot. Press the edge of the opening lightly to settle the worked edges.

6. Turn the garment through. Place the pocket inner part to the stitched pocket part, right sides together, pin around the outer. With a 1.5cm (⁵⁄₈in) seam allowance, join only the pocket pieces together by straight stitching around the circumference taking care not to stitch through the skirt fabric. Zigzag stitch around the outside of the straight stitch and trim away excess. Repeat for the other pocket. Press pocket well from both sides.

EMBELLISHING

THERE ARE LOTS OF WAYS TO FINISH OFF A MAKE, AS WE'VE TOUCHED ON IN THIS CHAPTER, YOU CAN USE A VARIETY OF WAYS TO TURN A HEM, JOIN A SEAM OR HIDE AN UNSIGHTLY RAW EDGE. BUT SOMETIMES YOU JUST NEED A LITTLE SOMETHING EXTRA. SO WHY NOT TRY APPLYING BIAS BINDING AS AN EDGING, SOME DIFFERENT BUTTONS, DECORATE A BUTTONHOLE OR PERHAPS EVEN ADD A LITTLE LACE TO A HEM LINE OR AS AN INSERTED PANEL?

buttons

bias binding

lace

LACE EDGING

What was once an extremely time-consuming item to produce and therefore very costly to purchase has become a more everyday addition, not just for lingerie or bridal gowns. If you have a look around most haberdasheries, you'll find a plethora of different styles, weights, colours, widths and qualities of lace.

Due to its light-weight construction, lace edging can be applied to almost any fabric type, but is most suited to light- to medium-weights. A lace finish has the magical ability to take a simple top or skirt and transform it into something wholly more elegant and flowing. Why not give it a try?

To apply lace really couldn't be easier to do. Stitch along the flat finished edge if it has one, or if not then on the sturdiest part of the lace. This avoids any unwanted damage to the more finely constructed parts.

See me transform a top with a simple lace edging on pages 116–117.

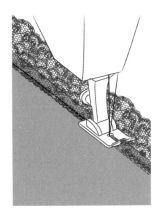

BIAS BINDING

Bias binding is a great invention and very occasionally my saviour. It can bring life and colour to a garment and also give a durable finish.

It is constructed by cutting strips of fabric diagonally across the grain line, otherwise known as on the bias, and joining them. Cutting diagonally gives stretch and bounce – which means that you can gently pull it to fit a curved edge. You can use bias binding to encapsulate one or more raw edges, say on an armhole or neck edge, or better still as a Hong Kong seam inside a jacket. You could also use it as an inward facing to a pair of trousers or a skirt, or along a hem edge to add flare or weight.

Bias binding can be used on most weights of fabric, although I'd suggest you pick something similar to your main fabric or better still make some from the same fabric.

I show you how to make your own bias binding and use it to finish a top on pages 118–119.

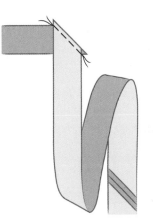

BUTTONS & BUTTONHOLES

Buttons come in all shapes, sizes and styles, and are a really fantastic way to make something look truly individual. When applying buttons, its best to use a fabric stabilizer behind the button stand and also the buttonhole to stop the closing from being pulled out of shape when under tension.

Most modern machines have a separate foot attachment to assist in stitching the right size hole for your button. Perhaps try using a complementary thread that picks out a different colour in your garment to bring attention to the buttonhole rather than disguise it? Buttons can be used on any fabric type and weight – the only limit will be your machine's ability to stitch the hole.

See how buttons can transform a simple skirt on pages 110–111 and how to add a unique finish to the buttonholes and buttons on a jacket on pages 112–115.

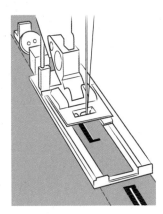

NAUTICAL-STYLE SKIRT

adding buttons

It's the finer details that give a garment its style and identity. Over the years styles fall in and out of fashion, but there are a few staples that live on and can stand the test of time. Military and nautical styles are great examples of this, signified by a defined garment edge and polished metalwork.

By adding a few extra finishing flourishes to an existing garment you can dramatically change its identity. In this alteration the finishing touches come in the form of 6 gold buttons. When added to a dark navy blue skirt they recreate the look of a sailor's high-waisted uniform.

WHAT YOU'LL NEED
Skirt • Tailor's chalk • Ruler or tape measure • Scissors or rotary cutter • Pins • Matching thread • 6 brass or gold buttons • Sewing machine • Hand-sewing needle

SHORTENING THE SKIRT

To make things a little more interesting I will also talk you through how to shorten a skirt using a double-folded hem. However, if your skirt is the right length for you feel free to skip this part.

1. Decide on your finished hemline and mark with chalk. Press the garment and lay it out flat. Now add a further 2.5cm (1in) for the seam allowance and mark out a line across the width of the garment. Cut neatly along the line.

   Optional: If the skirt section has a split in it, as the one I was working on did, turn through to the inside and pin along the centre back seam. Join this back seam together with a straight stitch, continuing past the desired hemline, backstitching at either end. Press the seam open.

2. To create the double-turned hem, fold the hemline upwards to the inside of the bottom edge by 5mm (¼in), and press well. Make the second fold, this time by 2cm (¾in), and press well. Pin to secure the hemline. Stitch from the right side on a 1.5cm (⁵⁄₈in) seam allowance. Secure the thread ends with a backstitch.

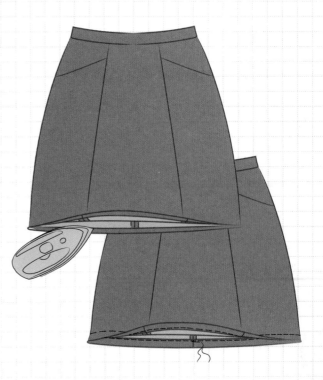

APPLYING THE BUTTONS

For the nautical look, 6 buttons work best. The Forces are all about precision, so that is exactly what we are going to achieve.

1. Measure a central line from the waistband to the hemline, either in chalk or with long basting stitches. Working from this line, evenly space out 6 button placements and mark with the chalk.

2. With your needle and thread join the first button to the garment by stitching carefully from the right side through the front skirt panel. Bring the needle back up through the fabric close to your first stitch, passing the needle through the first hole in the back of the button and drawing through the thread. Pass the needle back down on the diagonal hole and through into the fabric again. Do this in an alternating order between the four holes; five times on each pair will be plenty. On the last time wrap the thread tightly a few times around the threads behind the button and pass the needle back down through the fabric.

3. On the wrong side, tie off the thread by making a stitch through the existing stitches. Thread the needle through the loop and then pull tight. Do this at least twice and then trim off the excess. Repeat for each button and your skirt is ready to wear.

Adding buttons would also work fantastically well on a pair of high-waisted trousers or even to a classic-cut dress for a military officer's look.

CUSTOMIZING A JACKET
buttons and buttonholes

There's life in old clothes, even if you don't always feel inspired by them anymore. I must admit every now and again I love going for a rummage around a charity shop and seeing what little gems are tucked away on the rails. Occasionally there's something that with a little love can be transformed into something much fresher and up to date.

This is a great example of how a few simple customizations can make a huge difference to an old jacket. We're going to restitch the existing buttons, change a few of them for something different and liven up a few buttonholes.

WHAT YOU'LL NEED
Jacket to customize • Contrasting thread • Hand-sewing needle • Tailor's chalk or a chalk pencil • New buttons • Scissors • Seam ripper

BUTTONHOLE EMBELLISHMENT

A fantastic but really simple way to liven up a jacket is to restitch a few of the buttonholes in a contrasting thread. This works equally well on either a man's or a lady's jacket, and can be just a subtle twist or more of a statement with a high-contrast thread.

The front and lapel buttonholes of my jacket are working ones, however the cuff buttonholes are false. A standard buttonhole is constructed in one go by machine, made up of lots of small zigzag stitches along the long edges, with a larger zigzag at each end. The unstitched centre line is then cut open just big enough to allow a button through. On higher-end garments or tailor-made jackets the buttonholes are cut first and then the raw edges are handstitched.

You have two options here: you can either cut away the existing thread from the buttonhole or just stitch over the top of it. I chose to do the latter. You could use a thicker thread for this part, or just double up a standard thickness thread in your needle – this will help cover the existing stitching.

1. If you are doing this on a false buttonhole, remove the button before starting to sew. Taking the contrasting threaded needle, knotted at the end, begin at one end of the existing buttonhole.

2. From the reverse side of the fabric stitch up through and back down through the centre of the buttonhole.

3. Slowly work along the buttonhole one stitch at a time until you have covered the existing stitches. Finally tie off the thread ends.

As you may have worked the fabric a bit a light press with a warm iron around the buttonhole will help bring it back into shape. Make sure not to use steam if the jacket is made of wool.

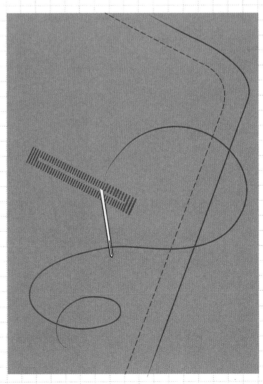

CHANGING THE BUTTONS

Normally, with a gent's jacket, the buttons are designed to not be too noticeable. I'm happy with that, but want to add a bit of a twist. On the 4 sleeve buttons I'm only going to replace the last button. Of course you could replace all of them, but I quite like the contrast that changing just one gives. That said, I am going to restitch all of the others with a different contrasting thread.

1. Begin by removing all the buttons from the outside, marking with tailor's chalk exactly where they were placed. On this jacket the buttons were stitched through the outer placket of the sleeve through a false buttonhole and into the inner placket. Mark both of these places for each button.

2. Take needle threaded with contrasting thread and working from the back of the outer placket bring the needle up and through the fabric at the position marked for the button placement.

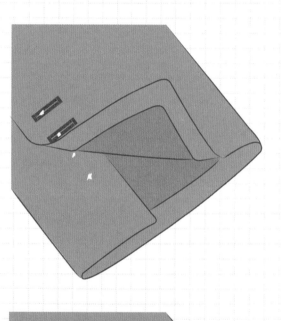

3. Thread the button onto the needle and pass back down through the diagonally opposite hole, and through the outer placket. Once the needle and thread are pulled through completely, I then pass the needle behind a few threads of the inner placket at the button mark, and draw the thread through fully. This brings the button close to the cuff and also the two plackets together. On passing the thread back up through, make sure to stitch the opposing holes in the button so that it creates a crossed stitch using all four holes.

4. Continue to stitch the holes, alternating between the diagonally opposite pairs. Do this a total of 5 to 6 times for each, giving a nice sturdy attachment. On the final stitch, before pulling the thread all the way through, pass the needle through the loop which has been created and pull tight, and then once more to knot and then cut the thread near to the base. Repeat this for all four buttons on each sleeve. I chose to swap the last button for a brass button and restitch the buttonhole with a contrasting thread, just as an extra statement.

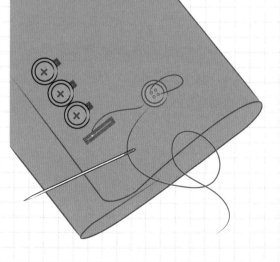

Why not give it a try? Have a rummage through your wardrobe or the local charity shop and see what you can make your own.

ENHANCING A VEST TOP

lace edging

Traditionally lace was used on celebration gowns such as wedding dresses, but there is absolutely no reason why you can't add a little splash of beauty to everyday plain garments.

While you can hand stitch lace, most lace can be joined to a garment with a straight stitch by machine. It's important to stitch along the most solid part of the lace pattern – this gives a stable join between the two parts. Also, it's best to choose the closest-matching thread colour you can; that way the lace will look like it was always there.

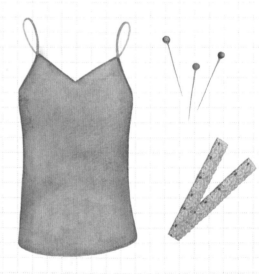

WHAT YOU'LL NEED
Vest top • Tape measure • Lace trim in your chosen colour • Scissors • Pins • Matching thread • Sewing machine • Tailor's mannequin (*optional*)

1. Measure the neckline and cut a length of lace 7cm (3in) longer than this, to allow the ends to be folded under neatly. Lay the top out on a flat surface with all shoulder straps laid upwards. Fold the lace in half, trying to match any pattern as you do so. Lay the lace along one half of the neckline, with the fold at the centre point. Place a pin pointing straight down at the neck edge point.

2. Take the lace to the sewing machine. Beginning in the centre of the lace where you have pinned, with a slow straight stitch begin to sew in same direction as the pin. Once you have almost reached the edge leave the needle in the down position, raise the presser foot and turn the lace 180° and put the presser foot back down. Now sew outwards towards the opposite side, turn again and sew back to the centre. Tie off thread ends. Open out the stitched lace section and lightly press. You can cut away the excess, although this is not strictly necessary.

3. Take your lace and lay out flat along the neck edge of the garment, being sure to match the points if you have a V neck, and matching the desired edge finish line. Pin the lace to the neck edge. Join the lace to the neck edge with a straight stitch. I recommend beginning in the middle and work outwards towards the shoulder straps. This will ensure that the points of the V neck stay aligned and don't move. Stitch up until the point where the neck edge meets the shoulder straps. Tie off thread ends.

4. Now, either try the top on or place it on a mannequin if you have one available. Fold the excess lace under itself to the wrong side, keeping the lace on top of the straps, and align the folded lace edge so it lines up with the outermost edge of the shoulder strap. Pin in place. Beginning from the neckline stitch upwards along the shoulder strap. Tie off thread ends.

This has made a plain top a little more special wouldn't you say? If you'd like to you can also add lace around the waist hemline:

5. Measure around the bottom hemline and add 10cm (4in). Leaving 5cm (2in) at either end, begin on one of the side seams to pin the lace around the hemline, matching edges as required. Starting 2.5cm (1in) from the side seam, straight stitch around the hemline to join the lace to the garment. Stop 2.5cm (1in) before you get to the original side seam. Turn the two parts of excess lace to the wrong side and pin together where they meet. Join the two lace parts with a straight stitch, carefully tying off thread ends and trimming thread excess. Finish joining the lace to the hem as before.

DECORATIVE EDGE FINISH

bias binding

If you get a piece of cotton and try pulling it in different directions, across gives a bit but not much. Lengthways gives even less, but diagonally gives a really good stretch and bounce. Bias binding harnesses this useful quality of the fabric, and allows you to manipulate it to fit a curved shape beautifully while leaving the main fabric relaxed. In doing so you can enclose an edge, whether it is raw or finished, without getting any unsightly puckers or creases.

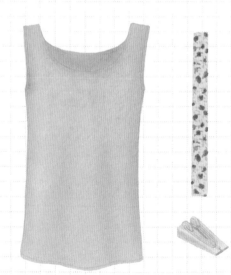

WHAT YOU'LL NEED
Vest top • Decorative cotton fabric for binding • Tape measure • Pins • Matching thread • Scissors • Bias-binding tool • Sewing machine • Bias-binding foot

TO MAKE YOUR OWN BIAS BINDING

1. Cut long strips of fabric diagonally, 2.5cm (1in) wide. Place the strips right sides together and at a 90° angle to each other. Straight stitch across the angle where they overlap, tying off thread ends. Trim back the excess and press open the seam.

2. If you are using a bias-binding tool, pass the strips of fabric through, pressing well as it comes out. (These tools are very cheap to buy online or from haberdashers.) Use a pin to help start it off. Or, if you are making this by hand, fold in the long raw edges of both sides equally until they almost meet in the centre and press the folded edges well.

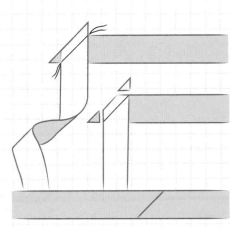

TO EDGE-STITCH BINDING TO A GARMENT

1. Fit the adjustable bias-banding foot onto your machine. Taking your bias binding, offer up one end of it into the foot opening. Using the winder or thumbscrew on the foot adjust so that the binding can feed through but not move side to side. The needle placement will be close to the open edge of the bias tape.

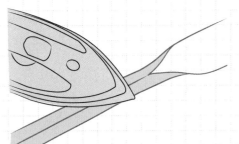

2. Now take the garment that you want to add the bias tape to. Begin with a lead of between 1.5– 2.5cm (½–1in) of bias tape and feed in your fabric to the centre part of the foot. This should sandwich the garment in between the folds of the bias tape.

3. Once happy with the placement, lower the presser foot and adjust the needle position if required. Begin stitching slowly with a straight stitch on your preferred length. I opted for 2.2. Continue all the way around until you are about 2.5cm (1in) from where you started. Take the garment and bias tape out of the foot and swap it for a standard foot. Trim back the leading excess bias tape close to your first stitches.

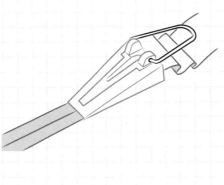

4. Trim the other end of your bias tape so that it extends past the start by 1.5cm (½in). Fold this excess under and pin in place – this will create the appearance of a continuous binding. Edge stitch the remainder as neatly as you can to the garment, removing the pins as you go. Repeat the process for any other edges you want to trim, such as around the sleeve holes.

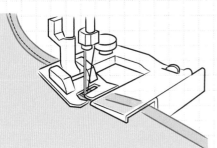

Now give it a good press and go show it off.

BOW TIE

SLEEVELESS BLOUSE

INFINITY SCARF

SCUBA SKIRT

SUNDAY SWEATSHIRT

PYJAMA TROUSERS

SUMMER DRESS

MAKE IT FROM SCRATCH

Not everything needs a pattern - sometimes you really can make a garment just from your own body measurements. Nothing quite beats making a garment from just fabric, a needle and some thread.

BOW TIE

show a little personal flair

Putting on a nice outfit and getting all dressed up makes you feel great, doesn't it? Well it's no different for chaps, but the chances to express yourself and wear a bit of colour is normally a bit limited, quite often only to socks and cuff links. Well, why not try making this colourful bow tie?

Hand-tied bow ties can be tricky to sew, let alone tie, but this project is a recipe for success: using a press stud at the back allows for quick and easy fastening. The beauty of this is that you don't need a pattern; this make just requires a few measurements.

You might be interested to know that the bow tie originated from the mercenary soldiers of Croatia during the 17th century, as a method for keeping the neck of their shirts together. This was subsequently adopted by the upper classes of France, adapted into a form that we now see on the high street. Traditionally the bow tie was made from silks or satins, however over more recent years fashion has broken free from these constraints and many can now be found made from cotton, linen or even wool.

- -

WHAT YOU'LL NEED
Fabric (silk, satin, linen, light- to medium-weight cotton)
• Measuring tape • Iron-on fusible interfacing *(optional)*
• Chopstick • Pins • Matching thread • Sewing machine
• Hand-sewing needle • Tailor's chalk • Sew-on press stud

TO MAKE THE BOW TIE

1. Begin by taking the measurement for the neck around the outside of the upturned collar of one of your shirts. If you're making the tie as a gift you could of course just over estimate the size and adjust the press stud later to get the correct fit.

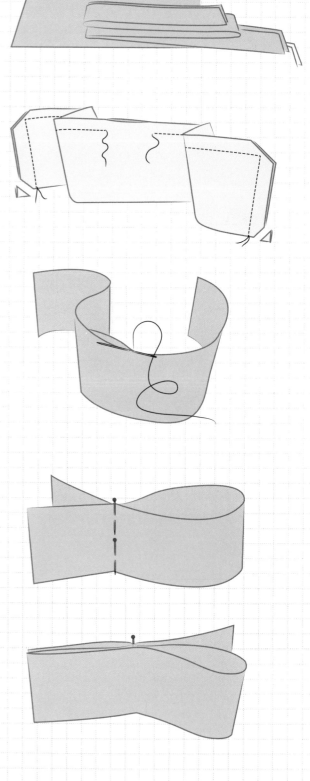

2. Give your chosen fabric a really good press, testing on a small hidden section first to get the correct heat setting. Then measure and cut out four pieces of fabric:

1 x bow tie main section: 13.5 x 38.5cm (5¼ x 15¼in)
1 x knot section: 10 x 8.5cm (4 x 3½in)
2 x band section: The neck measurement plus an additional 5 x 4cm (2 x 1½in)

Tip: If you are using a particularly soft silk or satin you may wish to stabilize the fabric with an iron-on fusible interfacing on the wrong side. This gives a little more rigidity to the bow once made.

3. Taking the main section, fold over widthways matching the raw edges. Press lightly and pin around the outer edge. Mark a 4–5cm (1½–2in) gap in the middle of the long raw edge. Your piece should measure 6.75 x 38.5cm (3 x 15¼in).

4. Beginning on the folded edge, with a 1.5cm (⅝in) seam allowance, stitch down the short edge, stopping 1.5cm (⅝in) before the corner point. Leaving the needle down though the fabric, raise the presser foot and turn the fabric 90° then lower the presser foot. Continue stitching up until the first mark then place a backstitch. Raise both the needle and presser foot.

5. Restart stitching at the second mark, turning the corner as you did at step 4. Trim back seam allowances and clip the corners, making sure not to cut the stitch line. Turn through the gap to the right side, working out the seams and corners fully and lightly press. Using a hand needle and thread, slipstitch the gap closed.

6. Take the knot section and assemble as you did for the main section, this time leaving a 2cm (¾in) centre gap.

7. Fold the main bow tie section in half lengthways. Measure a third in from the non-folded end and pin vertically. Open the ends and the looped section, then flatten out so the pinned line is in the centre. Check the non-stitched ends meet the folded parts; adjust if necessary. Open out and straight stitch along the pin line, backstitching or tying off threads at beginning and end.

8. Open out the ends, again opening the loop, laying flat to bring the line of stitching to the middle. To secure, place a couple of stitches to hold the previous stitch line central on the loop.

9. Fold the bow in half widthways, and then the upper and lower parts back on themselves to create a W pleated shape. Take the knot section and wrap this around the bow section, pin in place. Use a slipstitch to secure the knot to itself.

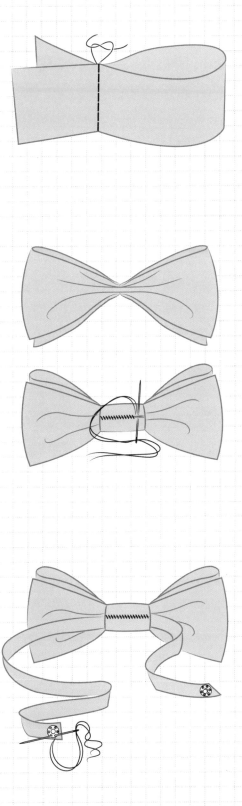

TO MAKE THE NECKBAND

1. Take the two long sections and match right sides together. Cut to a point at one end. Beginning at the squared end, and using the width of your presser foot as a seam allowance guide, join the two parts together with a straight stitch, turning corners as you did before, leaving an unstitched opening at the squared end. Trim back the seam allowance and carefully clip the corners.

2. Using a chopstick or similar tool, turn the band through the open end by very gently pushing the pointed end up inside the band, working along slowly. Once turned through fully, press well. You can either hand stitch or machine stitch the open end closed.

3. Pass the band through the back of the knot section, using the chopstick to help ease it through. Check for fit and mark on both ends of the neckband where you'd like the press stud to be.

APPLYING THE PRESS STUD

1. Make a mark on the inner face of the neckband pointed end, equally in from the edges and the point itself. Place the female part of the press stud on the mark and, using needle and thread, secure to the fabric by stitching through the outer holes equally. Sew through one layer of the fabric rather than both. If you're able to try the bow tie on to get a correct fitting now is the time. According to your fitting, check your mark on the opposing face of the inner neckband part.

Tip: Check the fabric is flat and not twisted – you don't want to apply the press stud to the wrong side.

2. Take the male part of the press stud and secure this to your neckband inner on top of the mark. Again stitch around the outer perimeter holes through just one layer of the fabric. Finally, test that the female and male parts of the press stud marry up and work as intended.

SLEEVELESS BLOUSE

a pretty top from a free-to-use pattern

Patterns and ways to source them have changed massively over the years, and the digital age has been a huge catalyst. There are lots of patterns available to download from the internet, so you can instantly print one at home and get stitching within minutes of choosing. There are some sites that let you put in your measurements, choose a pattern and within an hour you have a made-to-measure pattern waiting for you.

This gorgeous summer blouse pattern, the Sorbetto from Colette, is a completely free online download so won't cost you a penny. It has two main sections to it, the front and back sections, and an optional extra of making your own bias binding for the neck and armholes. Bias binding in a matching fabric can be a great addition.

You can use many different fabric types to make this top, although I think it's best suited to a light-weight cotton, linen or viscose polyester.

- -

WHAT YOU'LL NEED
Printed pattern (colettepatterns.com/catalog/sorbetto) • Fabric (light-weight cotton, linen, viscose polyester) • Tailor's chalk • Matching thread • Sewing machine • Pins • Measuring tape • Bias- binding maker (if making your own bias tape)

PRINT AND ASSEMBLE

First of all you have to print out and assemble the pattern itself. This one only has 10 pages to it so doesn't take too long at all. You can either use glue sticks and overlap the pages or trim back the margins or use sticky tape to join them together. Both work equally well. Cut out the pattern for the desired size and place on your fabric, making sure to transfer all markings. Both sections require you cut out on the fold.

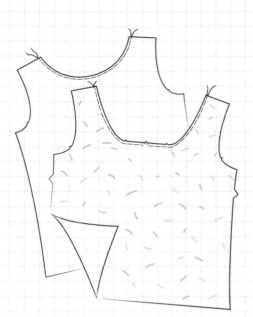

TO MAKE THE BLOUSE

If like me, you choose a light-weight cotton lawn for this make, it is important to stay stitch the neck edge. Stay stitching helps prevent the garment getting skewed and stretched out of shape when you are constructing.

1. To stay stitch, use a straight stitch setting and work from shoulder to shoulder on the front section, making sure to keep inside your seam allowance, which on the neck edge was 1.5cm (⅝in), so around 4mm (⅛in) would be ideal. These don't need to be tied off. Repeat this on the back section.

2. Take the blouse front and make up the darts by bringing the lines together, then pinning. To get a good finish stitch from the side towards the point of the dart. This helps avoid getting any puckers or gathers on the point. Tie the threads off at the point, do not backstitch. Press the darts downward towards the waist.

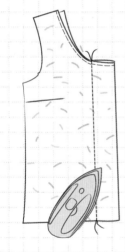

3. On the blouse front, with wrong sides together, bring the two pleat lines together and pin in place. With the right side facing you, carefully stitch down the pleat from neck edge to hem. Press the pleat stitches with the tip of your iron to set them, this helps them hold firm and not loosen. Try not to iron the centre of the pleat as you don't want a line running down the middle. On the right side of the blouse front, centre the pleat over the stitch line and press the pleat flat. Press again from the wrong side.

4. With a long stitch length, machine baste the top and bottom of the pleat inside of the seam allowances. Basting will help to hold the pleat in place over the rest of the construction.

Tip: It's okay to deviate from the pattern to add your own personal style. For example, I wanted to use a French seam to keep the inside as beautiful as the outside. These are my steps, if you like the standard seam you can follow the Colette instructions that come with the pattern.

5. With wrong sides together match notches. Using a straight stitch with a 5mm (¼in) seam allowance, join the blouse front to blouse back at shoulders and side seams. Trim back any excess fabric or loose threads from the material, then turn through so right sides are now together. Work the seams out fully by rolling them gently between your forefinger and thumb, lightly press and pin. Now with an 8mm (⅜in) seam allowance, stitch around all seams again.

6. Press seams to one side. Turn through and press. You'll see that now all of your raw edges have been tidied up on the inside of the French seam. I think this is a beautiful way to finish a garment that you want to feel good on the inside.

7. I also made bias tape in the same fabric for the neck and armhole edges. If you'd like to see how, go to page 119. Unfold the bias tape completely and matching the top raw edges, pin it all around the neckline, with the blouse turned inside out, so the right side of the bias tape is facing the wrong side of the garment. Leave a gap of 5cm (2in) at the back centre of the neckline, and 7cm (3in) of bias tape trailing on each side.

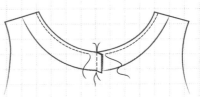

8. Stitch the bias tape around the neckline, stopping when you reach the gap. The bias tape should be unfolded, and you'll be stitching along the crease nearest the neck edge. Take the two ends of the bias tape and pinch them together with right sides together, leaving enough room to cover the gap. Pin in place and adjust the pin until the bias tape is the right length.

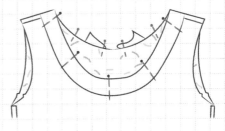

9. Stitch the ends together at the point that you pinned them. Trim the excess bias tape ends and press this small seam in the bias tape open. Stitch the bias tape to the neckline across the gap that you left. You should now have the bias tape joined in a complete circle around the neckline.

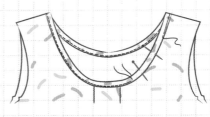

10. Turn the blouse through the right way and with it turn the bias tape to the outside, tucking under the remaining fold that runs along the length of the bias tape. Pin this in place. Edge stitch the bias tape to the neckline, close to the fold. Use this same technique (steps 7–10) to finish each of the armholes.

11. To create a narrow hem, turn the hem 5mm (¼in) to the wrong side, and press. Turn again 8mm (⅜in) and press. Stitch the hem in place with a straight stitch.

There you have it - a beautiful blouse that has cost you nothing more than a few sheets of paper and the fabric you chose.

INFINITY SCARF

easy techniques to transform a length of fabric

If you haven't undertaken a project from scratch yet, then with the help of this infinity scarf make I'm going to give you the courage to turn half a metre (yard) of fabric into a fantastic wearable garment. If on the other hand you've already conquered a few projects and you have an ever-growing fabric stash that needs a bit of a cull, then this is the perfect way to create some much-needed space, with the added benefit that it'll give you a reason to go fabric shopping!

I promise when you have made this scarf once, you'll be knocking up a new one with the change of the season. For this make you can use various fabric weights: cottons or viscose for spring and summer, and light knits or jerseys for autumn and winter. The instructions are the same no matter what the fabric choice.

WHAT YOU'LL NEED
50cm (20in) fabric (ideally 150cm/60in wide to allow a double wrap) • Ruler • Scissors or rotary cutter • Pins • Matching thread • Sewing machine • Hand-sewing needle

TO MAKE THE SCARF

1. Begin by pressing a section of fabric, ideally measuring 150cm (60in) across by 50cm (20in) long. This will allow for a double wrap around. Fold the fabric in half, right sides together, matching the long raw edges. Pin all the way along this long edge leaving the short ends open.

2. With a matching thread, begin straight stitching on a 1.5cm ($^5/_8$in) seam allowance along the pinned long edge. Remove the pins as you go. Either backstitch or tie off the threads at the beginning and end to secure. Stitch a row of zigzag stitching within the seam allowance along the sewn long edge, to help preserve the seam during washing.

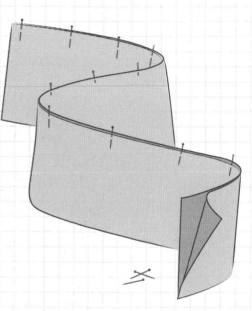

3. Next, slide your arm in through the centre opening. Take a light hold of the opposite end, pull this all the way through. You'll end up having the scarf turned through the correct way so you will be seeing the right side of the fabric.

4. Take both of the open ends of the fabric. Align the previously sewn seams and begin pinning the raw edges together, you'll be able to pin about three-quarters of the way around.

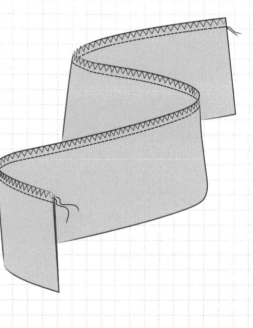

In this make you'll mostly use straight stitching on a machine, and you'll also get a chance to perfect your hand stitching to close up the final opening in the seam neatly.

5. Join the pinned raw edges, by sewing with a 1.5cm (⁵/₈in) seam allowance around as far as you can – this will be about three-quarters of the way around. Turn this sewn edge to the inside. You can do this either by working the fabric through the unsewn gap or by gently pulling on either end of the right sides. Once all the stitching is turned to the inside, press the opening so that the seam allowance is even with the previously sewn section.

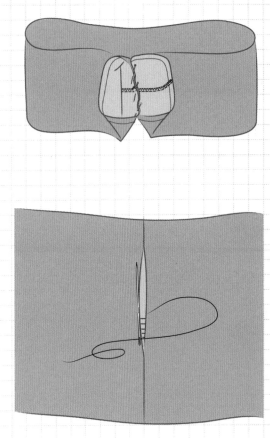

6. To close the gap we're going to use a type of slipstitch that's also known as a ladder stitch. Take a threaded needle, knotted at the end. Bring the needle through from the inside of the scarf at the end of the opening. Try to come through exactly on the pressed fold. Move the needle along just a few threads from where you first brought it out. Slip it back into the fabric and then slide it along inside of the fold just a few millimetres (fractions of an inch). Bring the needle out again on the fold line, drawing the thread all the way out. Slip the needle into the fabric on the opposite fold. Slide the needle along by a few more millimetres (fractions of an inch) and bring it out on the pressed fold.

7. Repeat this 'in, along, out, across' method all the way along the opening. After every few stitches gently pull on your threads to bring the folded edges together perfectly. Once you reach the end of the opening tie off with a securing stitch and trim away any excess thread.

Give the scarf a really good press on all sides, especially on the stitched seams. That's it, you're all done! You can experiment with tying your scarf in lots of different knots.

SCUBA SKIRT

no pattern required – just cut to fit

Sometimes there is nothing better than creating a garment from scratch with nothing but some fabric, a tape measure and a threaded sewing machine. With this box-pleated skirt project you don't even need a pattern.

The beauty of this skirt is that you can choose various weights of fabric and get completely different styles each time with fantastic results. The box pleating gives a great shape to an otherwise plain garment. Using a fabric like scuba can create a very modern-looking skirt that holds a great shape and as it has a stretch – no zip is needed.

During this project I'm going to take you through the steps to create a boxed pleat, a straight seam, a waistband and a single-turned hem.

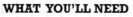

WHAT YOU'LL NEED
Fabric (scuba or a structured stretch is ideal) • Measuring tape • Matching thread • Tailor's chalk • Scissors • Pins • Sewing machine

TO MAKE THE SKIRT

1. Give your fabric a good press. Scuba can have slightly different finishes and may need a different heat setting, so it's best to test out on a small hidden section first.

   Begin by taking down some important measurements.
   – Waist
   – Hip
   – Waist to desired hemline

   Taking your waist to hemline measurement, subtract 2cm (³⁄₄in). Measure and mark this depth across the full width of your fabric from selvedge to selvedge. Cut out the fabric accordingly – you should be left with a rectangle of fabric.

   Tip: If you need a wider section you can cut another piece to the same depth and join the two sections together on the short edge with a straight stitch. Then just treat this as one whole piece.

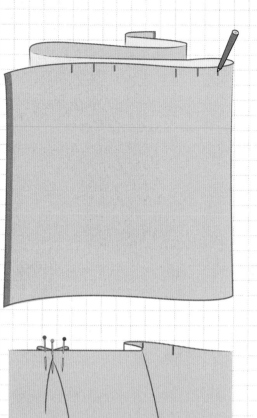

2. Now it's time to construct the pleats. You can make the pleats whatever depth you desire. I created a 2.5cm (1in) box pleat every 7cm (3in). Working from one selvedge to the other, leave a 7cm (3in) gap, then with tailor's chalk make 3 small marks each 2.5cm (1in) apart. Again leave a gap of 7cm (3in) and then repeat the three marks. Continue this measuring and marking across the width of the fabric.

3. For each pleat, take the two outer marks and bring them inwards to meet the middle mark, then pin in place. Continue to do this until you have a pinned skirt section equal to or more than your desired waist measurement. Using a long stitch length, baste each of the pleats in place with a 1.5cm (⁵⁄₈in) seam allowance, removing the pins as you do so. Press the top few inches of each pleat to help them hold their shape.

4. To create the waistband, take the waist and hip measurements and subtract 4cm (1½in) from each. Lay out the fabric and mark out this new waist measurement. Leave a depth of 9cm (3½in) then mark out the new hip measurement parallel to the waist mark. This will leave you a rectangle with two slightly slanted ends, depending on the difference in waist to hip. Cut out two of the waistband pieces.

5. Place the waistband sections right side to right side, pinning together along the upper waist edge. Using a stretch stitch, join waistband sections along the pinned waist edge, open flat and press the seam to one side.

6. Lay the waistband out flat on top of the pleated skirt section, right sides together, matching top raw edges of the skirt and the waistband hip edge and pin. Using a stretch stitch again, join the waistband to the skirt section. Press the seam upwards towards the waistband.

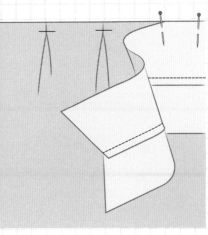

7. Lay the skirt out flat, right side up with the waistband opened out. Fold the skirt in half lengthways, right sides together to match the raw back seam edges and pin in place. Close the back seam with a straight stitch, securing thread ends with a backstitch or knot at the beginning and end.

8. Fold down the uppermost waistband section and try the skirt on. If you feel that it needs adjustment, just restitch inside the previous stitch line.

9. Trim away any excess from the back seam to approximately 8mm (³⁄₈in) from the stitch line and press open. With the uppermost waistband folded down, turn under 6mm (¹⁄₄in) so that the folded edge is just below the waistband seam and pin in place. This encases all the raw edges on the inside of the waistband.

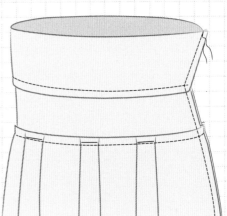

10. Working from the outside, straight stitch carefully on the original waistband seam, making sure you catch the folded-under waistband inner as you stitch. Remove the pins as you go.

Tip: As scuba has a reasonable amount of structure and it doesn't fray we are just going to do a single-turned hem so that we don't add too much bulk.

11. To hem, turn under and lightly press 2cm (³⁄₄in) of the lower raw edge and pin in place. You may want to clip the corner of the end of the back seam so that when folded up it doesn't peek out at all. From the right side of the skirt stitch slowly on a 1.5cm (⁵⁄₈in) seam allowance from the back seam around the circumference.

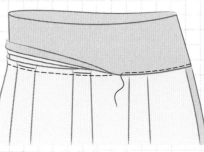

You now have a really versatile box-pleated skirt that you've created just from measurements, fabric and your trusty machine, with no need for a paper pattern.

SUNDAY SWEATSHIRT

made-to-measure comfort

The inspiration for this top came from a photo of a poncho-style top. My mind then started considering different fabrics, and if I was to recreate it how the fabric choices might alter the style. This is the process that I enjoy the most: exploring the endless possibilities, whittled down to your favourite.

I selected a sweatshirt material for this make. It gives a nice relaxed, some may say slouchy, shape and is pretty easy and forgiving to work with. You could also use a T-shirting or jersey fabric, for spring or summer wear.

We won't be using a pattern for this project, but instead a few vital measurements. During this make I will guide you through the process of measuring and drafting the garment, sewing straight sections with an over-edge stitch, a single-turned hem, and we will also create buttonholes and attach buttons.

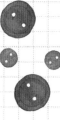

WHAT YOU'LL NEED
150cm (60in) sweatshirt fabric • Ruler (a French curve ruler is ideal too if you have one) • Tailor's chalk • Fabric scissors or rotary cutter • Pins • Bulldog clips • Matching or contrasting thread (depending on whether you want an obvious stitch or not) • 4 buttons • Sewing machine • Buttonhole foot • Hand-sewing needle

DRAFTING YOUR PATTERN

1. To draft your top, begin by drawing out on the wrong side of your fabric; this just takes a little bit of planning and calculations, but nothing too tricky I promise. You could of course use pattern paper to draft onto and then transfer to your fabric: I'll leave this up to you.

First measure:
– Waist
– Nape (the back of the neck) to hem edge
– Neck edge to sleeve hem
– Preferred sleeve width

Take your waist measurement, add 25cm (10in) and then halve the total. Lay out your fabric right side down. With your tailor's chalk and a ruler centrally mark out your lower hemline according to your newly calculated waist measurement. Include a 1.5cm (⅝in) seam allowance on all sides, and most importantly allow an additional 25cm (10in) at either end for the sleeves. Mark the centre point of this hemline.

For example, I made this top for a 85cm (34in) waist, so my measurement was 85cm + 25cm / 2 + 25cm + 25cm = 105cm. (34in + 10in / 2 + 10in + 10in = 42in)

2. From the centre point of the hemline, measure at a right angle your waist to nape measurement, then add 1.5cm (⅝in) to this point and mark. Measure outwards each way from this central neck edge point 14cm (5½in) and up 3.5cm (1½in). Draw a smooth curve to join these three points. A French curve ruler is ideal for this. If you don't have one just start shallow from the centre and steepen the curve at the outer points. From these outer points, measure the desired sleeve length, adding on 1.5cm (⅝in). Drop by 7cm (3in) and mark: this is to angle the sleeves down from the neck line.

3. Next we need to mark out the sleeve – this is just the sleeve width measurement marked at right angles to the hem line. Make a small mark at the desired sleeve width, but actually carry on this line all the way to the hemline.

4. You should have two rectangle shapes with one edge having a protruding shoulder/neck line shape to it (see the sketch). If that's not the case, don't panic, just slowly walk back through the measurements and markings above to see if anything was missed.

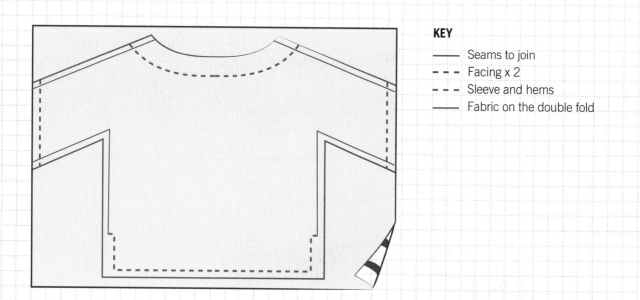

KEY

———— Seams to join
– – – Facing x 2
- - - Sleeve and hems
———— Fabric on the double fold

5. Once you're happy, cut out two of these shapes, pattern matching if required. If you're not pattern matching it's easiest to do this on doubled over fabric. Using the bulldog clips or pins, join the outer edges of the two garment pieces, leaving the neck and armholes unclipped, and try it on for size. Double check that the waist and armholes have enough room – these can be easily moved in or out at this stage. Once happy, slip in a couple of pins to mark where it felt comfortable; remember we're going for a relaxed look. Carefully take the top off and, using your pins as a guide, mark out a further two lines for each of the arms, one straight up from the waist line side seam at the hemline, and one parallel to the angle of the upper sleeve, beginning at the sleeve lower point. Where these two meet is the armpit.

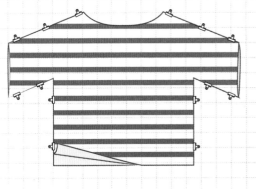

6. Before we finish this section, we just need to cut out a neck edge facing. Do this by copying the neck edge shape and the first 5–8cm (2–3in) of the garment. Cut out two of these and set to one side for now. Believe me when I say that this was the trickiest part of the whole make. If you've ended up with something looking like this give yourself a big pat on the back!

TO MAKE THE SWEATSHIRT

1. Lay out the two garment pieces, right sides together. Pin around the outer edge, except for the neck edge, armholes and waist edge. Make a mark on the side seam 16.5cm (6½in) up from the hemline. If your machine has this option, select an over-edge stitch. The beauty of this stitch is that it essentially does what an overlocker does, except the cutting bit. Which means you only have to go along the seams once to get a stitched edge that will also resist fraying. Of course, you can get this effect by doing a straight stitch followed by a zigzag stitch, but this is lots quicker.

2. Join the shoulder seams together with a 1.5cm (⅝in) seam allowance, securing thread ends by tying off or double stitching. Beginning on the arm lower edge, join together, pivoting the corner on the armpit by leaving the needle down, turning the garment and then stitching the side seams. Stop at the mark that you made on the side seam; this will make our placket sections for our buttons. Tie off or backstitch to secure thread ends.

3. Trim away the excess up to the edge of your over-edge stitches. Snip the armpit corner excess, being careful not to cut the stitches. For the placket parts cut downwards at a 45° angle towards the final stitch of the side seam, much like an arrow head. Press back and pin the plackets to the inside so that they follow the line of the side seam. These should be approximately 1.5cm (⅝in).

4. Stitch the plackets in place with a straight stitch. Begin on the hem edge, and stitch up to the top of the slit. Turn 90° and stitch across, then turn another 90° and stitch back down the opposite side. If you like you can strengthen the placket top edge by just going back over it.

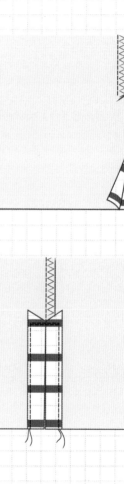

5. Fold upwards to the wrong side the lower hem edge by 2cm (³/₄in), press and pin. Straight stitch on a 1.5cm (⁵/₈in) seam allowance. Likewise fold inwards the sleeve edges by 2cm (³/₄in) and straight stitch with a 1.5cm (⁵/₈in) seam allowance.

6. Take your facing sections and place them right sides together. Join together on the short edges. Place the facing to the garment neck edge, right sides together, matching the shoulder seams, and pin in place. Join the facing to garment along the neck edge, trim excess and clip into the curve to allow it to sit flat.

7. Turn facing to the inside and press the neck edge from the inside, making sure the seam is worked out fully. Topstitch the neck edge on a 1.5cm (⁵/₈in) allowance to hold the facings in place to the inside.

8. Decide on your button placement on the side-seam plackets. Using your buttonhole setting make two buttonholes on one of the placket parts and a mirror image pair of buttonholes on the same placket part on the other side seam. Fix your buttons to the inside of the other placket parts. This enables the two parts to overlay one another and sit flat.

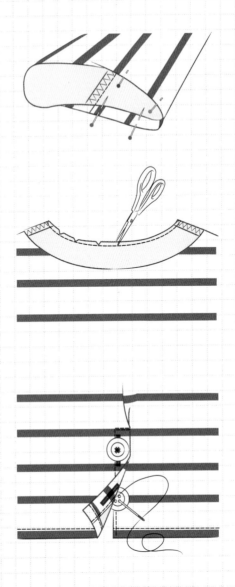

Now stand back and admire your self-drafted, no-pattern-required, Sunday morning sweatshirt. I hope you feel super proud - you certainly should be.

PYJAMA TROUSERS

make your own pattern from an old pair

I love the satisfaction you get when you've made something from just the materials of fabric and thread. Not everything you make has to be paraded out in public though; some items are just for wearing in the comfort of your own home.

We are going to make a fantastically easy pair of drawstring-waisted pyjama trousers. The pattern itself is going to be drafted by tracing from another pair of pyjamas. You could of course use a relaxed fit pair of trousers or jeans to get the same basic shape to work from – after all, patterns are just a guide.

We're going to step through the simple process of pattern drafting the pyjamas, the stitching and the threading of the waistband. I promise you in less than a couple of hours you'll have a brand-new pair to snuggle up in.

- -

WHAT YOU'LL NEED

For the pattern drafting: Dot and cross or pattern paper (or a few A3 sheets stuck together) • Pattern weights 2 pens/pencils Small piece of paper or card • Sticky tape or 2 x elastic bands

For the pyjamas: Cotton/brushed cotton – 2.5m (3yd) is plenty for adult men up to XL and 2m (6ft 5in) tall • Scissors or rotary cutter and mat • Pins • Matching thread • Sewing machine Buttonhole foot • Tailor's chalk • Seam ripper • Waistband drawstring cord • Safety pin

PATTERN TRACING

1. Begin by laying out your pattern paper on a flat even surface. Hopefully it's not creased; if it is just give it a quick iron on a medium heat setting (no steam).

2. Take your existing pyjamas and fold these in half on the waist, so that the fronts of the legs are together. Lay these out flat on top of the pattern paper and weigh down in place.

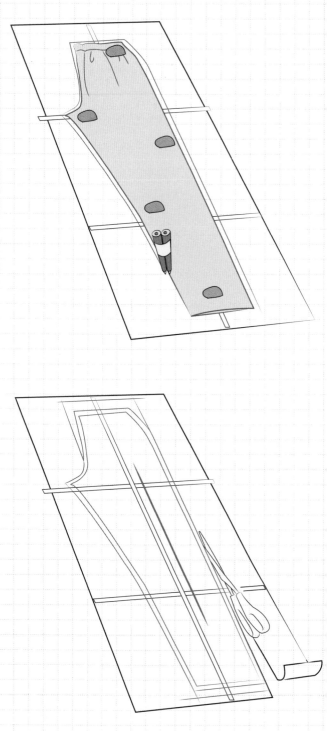

3. Take your two pencils/pens and place them side by side, check that the tips are 1.5cm (⁵⁄₈in) apart, which will be our seam allowance for this make. If you need to, use a folded piece of card or paper to increase the gap. Once you are happy, use sticky tape or elastic bands to hold them firmly together at the top and bottom. With both of the pencil tips touching the paper side by side, draw around the outer edge of the original trousers. You'll notice that as you trace the outline you are in turn marking a nice and even 1.5cm (⁵⁄₈in) seam allowance as you go.

4. To give us a decent hem we're going to extend out the ankle section by 4cm (1¹⁄₂in). To do this use your ruler to draw a straight parallel line 2.5cm (1in) below the original hemline (remember the seam allowance is automatically being added by your pencils). Extend the leg side seams to join up with this new hemline. Similarly, so that you have a good waistband portion to work with, extend the waistband top edge by 5cm (2in). While doing this, square off the top part of the trousers by drawing a line from the fullest part of the hip/seat up to the new waistband top edge and likewise from the same point on the front part up to the waistband.

5. Once you are happy that you have closely marked out the shape, you can take away the weights and the original trousers. Mark the grain line on the pattern, that is to say the direction of the fabric. This will help you to align the pattern if you wanted to use a striped or checked pattern. Cut out the paper pattern along your outer drawn line. Lay out your fabric, place the paper pattern on top matching your grain line to the pattern or running parallel to the selvedges, pin or weigh the pattern down to hold in place. Cut out four of the fabric sections.

Tip: If you want to speed things up, you can double over the fabric, wrong sides together, and that way cut out two at a time.

TO MAKE THE PYJAMAS

1. So now it's time to get making. Take two of the leg parts and, placing them right sides together, pin them along the inside leg seam, the part from the ankle up to the point of the crotch. Take this to your machine and with a matching thread, on a 1.5cm (⁵⁄₈in) seam allowance straight stitch along this seam. Follow this up with a zigzag within the seam allowance, to help reduce any fraying. Trim back any excess fabric, being careful not to cut the zigzag stitches. Do the same for the other two leg parts.

2. Open out the sewn leg parts and now place them one on top of the other, with right sides together. Pin around the centre seam. This is the front waist to back waist and when laid out looks like a big 'U' shape. Stitch this seam twice with a straight stitch, just to give it an extra bit of strength. Again neaten this edge by following up with a row of zigzag stitches within the seam allowance and trim away any excess fabric. Remember to be careful not to cut any stitches as you go.

3. Now shake the trousers out a bit and bring together the centre front and centre back seams, so that the right sides of the fabric are facing and the sewn seams are to the outside. Match the leg outer side seams for both legs and pin these in place. At this point take a moment to double check that they look like a pair of trousers. Believe me when you're first making trousers it's very easy to get a bit confused and stitch the wrong seams together! Join both of these outer leg seams, again by using our trusted straight stitch, followed by a zigzag within the seam allowance. Carefully trimming away any excess fabric.

4. Turn the trousers out the correct way. To hem the bottom of the trouser legs take one of the legs and press inwards to the wrong side with a seam allowance of 1.5cm (⁵⁄₈in), turn inwards and press again this time by 2.5cm (1in). Pin this in place ready for stitching. Beginning from either of the leg seams, straight stitch around the leg opening 2cm (³⁄₄in) in from the pressed hem edge. Backstitch or tie off threads ends and trim any excess threads. Do this for both legs.

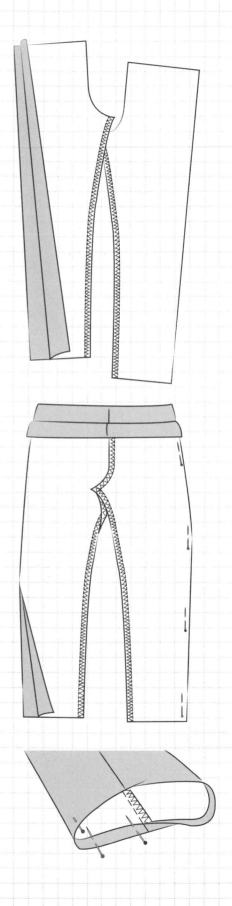

5. Okay, so the waistband is really just a large double turned section. To get this right we first have to make some markings.

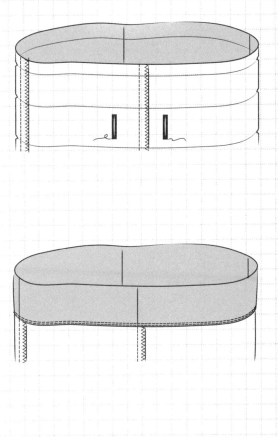

RAW EDGE: The first mark is 1.5cm (⁵⁄₈in) in from the raw edge of the waist.

UPPER WAISTBAND: The second is a further 3.5cm (1¹⁄₂in) down from the raw edge mark.

LOWER WAISTBAND: The third is another 3.5cm (1¹⁄₂in) from the upper waistband mark.

BUTTONHOLES: Finally, mark out the two buttonholes. These are placed vertically between the upper and lower waistband marks, 2cm (³⁄₄in) either side of the centre front seam. These will be used for the drawstring.

6. From the right side of the fabric, use your buttonhole foot and a 1.5cm (⁵⁄₈in) button as a guide, stitch two vertical buttonholes in between the upper and lower waistband measurements you previously marked. To open these up, take a seam ripper and carefully cut the fabric between the stitched sides of the buttonhole.

Tip: To stop you from over running and cutting through the end stitches, place a pin in at each end.

7. Turn down and press the raw edge of the waistband, this should be to the 1.5cm (⁵⁄₈in) mark we made earlier. Turn down and press the second fold as per the upper waistband mark. Pin the waistband in place. Make a row of straight stitches just in from the waistband lower fold to secure in place. If you wish, you can place a second row of stitching parallel to the first. This will help the waistband to sit flat and makes it look more professional.

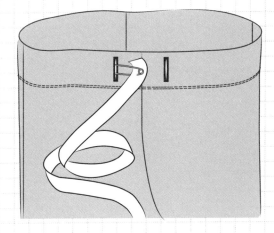

8. The last thing is to cut the drawstring to length. Depending on the type of drawstring you have chosen, you may choose to fold over and stitch the ends. Take a safety pin and secure this through one end of the drawstring. Slide the closed safety pin through one of the buttonhole openings and feed the drawstring all the way around the channel of the waistband, until you reach the other buttonhole opening. Pull the drawstring through and remove the safety pin.

It doesn't matter who you are making the PJs for: the same process applies to men's, women's and children's trousers.

SUMMER DRESS

downloadable pattern with personal sizing

Another great place I've found online for digital patterns is a site called lekala.co. The beauty of this is that you can find a pattern you like, enter your measurements and in a matter of hours (maybe minutes) you receive an email with a customized pattern for your size. So no more trying to blend different size upper and lower sections. You may also choose to either draw in or expand out the darts and seams as per your personal preference. Feel free – remember patterns are only guidelines not rules!

On this make you get to not only create a fantastic summer dress but also practise putting in a concealed side zip, plus work on joining a facing to make it look really professional.

You can choose from a multitude of fabrics for this dress, but I'd suggest to keep it nice and light for summer – a cotton with a slight stretch would be perfect.

WHAT YOU'LL NEED
Printed Lekala pattern 4263 (lekala.co/catalog/dresses/pattern/4263) • Fabric – cotton is perfect! • Tailor's chalk • Iron-on interfacing *(optional)* • Pins • Measuring tape • Matching thread • 2m/6¹/₂ft bias binding tape *(optional)* • Sewing machine • Concealed zip (23cm/9in) • Concealed zipper foot

PRINT AND ASSEMBLE PATTERN

First you'll need to print out and assemble the pattern. Make sure when you print you don't scale the size at all. There's a 10 x10cm (4 x 4in) test square on the last page to check your measurement; I suggest printing this page first. Once printed, you can either use glue sticks and overlap the pages or trim back the margins and use sticky tape to join them together. Both will work equally well.

Note: *The seam allowance for this pattern is 1cm (³⁄₈in), which is a little smaller than some commercial patterns.*

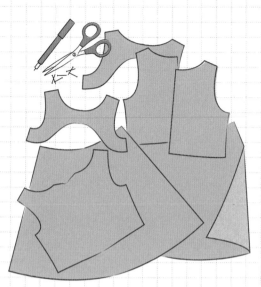

TO MAKE THE DRESS

1. Cut out the 6 paper pieces and place on top of your fabric. Transfer all markings and cut out: you should have 7 fabric pieces as you cut out 2 of the bodice back part. If you want to use an interfacing to stabilize the facings, cut out just the two facings in your chosen interfacing. Apply it to the wrong side of the facing fabric as per the manufacturer's guidelines.

2. Beginning with the front bodice sections, pin and sew the darts as per the pattern markings. Press the darts towards the centre.

Tip: Work from the widest part towards the point to get a nice finish with no puckers. Tie off the thread ends at the point rather than backstitching.

For the neckline there is a nice double inward pleat. Bring the two outer marks to meet the two inners, press the top 5cm (2in) and baste stitch within the seam allowance. Make up the back darts in the same manner as the front darts, pressing towards the centre.

3. Place the two upper back sections right sides together and join the centre back seam with a straight stitch. Neaten the raw edge with a zigzag or over-edge stitch and press to one side. Join the bodice front to the skirt front by placing right sides together, matching the raw waistline edges and straight stitching. Neaten the raw edge with a zigzag or over-edge and press upwards. Join the bodice back to the skirt back in the same way. Remember to finish the raw edge and press upwards.

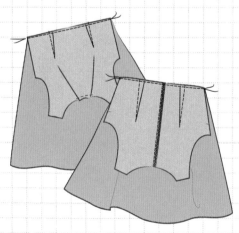

4. Zigzag stitch the left edges of both the dress front and back sections separately. Place the dress front and back sections together, right sides facing, matching notches and seams. Join together with a straight stitch from the left armhole to the first mark, then from the second mark all the way to the hem. Backstitch at beginning and end of each seam. Press open the seam allowances including the gap for the concealed zip.

5. Take the concealed zip, open it up fully, unfurl the teeth and press with the tip of a warm iron. Be sure not to melt the nylon teeth – test the iron on the bottom of the zip first. This helps with the stitching. Pin the opened zip right side to the inward pressed allowance of the gap in the side seam. Match the top stops of the zip to the top of the gap, and the seam allowance raw edges to the tape edges. With your concealed zipper foot fitted to your machine, place the unfurled teeth of the right-hand zipper tape into the left-most groove of the zipper foot. Carefully stitch from the top of the zip down as far as you can before you hit the body of the zip slider.

6. Now take the left-hand side of your zipper tape and place the unfurled teeth in the right-hand groove of the foot. Straight stitch from the top down as far as you can. Tie off thread ends and test the zip. Press the seam from the outside, being sure not to touch the teeth. If there is a gap at the base of the zip, pull the bottom of the closed zip away from the inside seam and stitch closed.

7. Swap back to your standard presser foot. With right sides together, match the right side seam raw edges and notches and join with a straight stitch. Zigzag stitch to neaten and press towards the back. With right sides together, match the raw edges of the shoulder seams and join with a straight stitch. Press these towards the back. Take your two facing sections, place them right sides together and join them on the shoulder seams and right side seam. Press open the seam allowances. Zigzag stitch the lower raw edge of the facings to neaten.

Optional: This next bit can be a little fiddly, so if you like you can use bias binding to join the facings along the neck edge and the armholes. Not only can this speed up your make but it can also be a great enhancement as you can add a contrasting colour.

8. If you're not using bias binding, place the facing right sides together with the dress bodice, matching raw neck edge and shoulder seams. Join with a straight stitch and clip into the seam allowance curve. Turn facing to the inside and press. Working from the inside, join the facing armholes to the dress armholes and clip into curves. Press. You could also do this with an edge stitch from the right side around the armholes.

9. The last thing to do is hem the dress with a single-turned hem to the inside, at your preferred length.

MAKE IT WEARABLE

Occasionally your clothing just needs some loving care or a spruce up to take it back to its former glory, so we may not be creating something new, but we are making something loved again.

Keeping up appearances

Today's modern world has become one where convenience rules, and that applies to clothing, too.

No longer do laces and silks have to be shipped in for your perusal before a garment is made. Now you can quite literally sit in the comfort of your own front room and browse away until you find that exact item you want, click, buy, have it delivered to your home and in some cases wear it out the very next day. Okay, not all bad I hear you say, and yes you're right – it is very convenient.

However, with ease of consumerism comes competition between retailers, cheaper prices and ultimately a more disposable mindset, whereby you can now buy trousers for less than it would cost you to gather the materials yourself, let alone make them. I'm not saying that they have no place, but I do wonder 'where's the fun in that?'

I'm keen for us to not slip completely into a consumer-led, throw-away society, and one of the cornerstones of *Make it, Own it, Love it* is to look after our clothes so they last a little longer. How to look after yourself and your kit was one of the early lessons that I was taught in the army. Upkeep of our clothing and equipment was one of the things that really got me into sewing. By making the odd running repair you can ensure your clothes look as good as new every time you wear them!

So what do you say - ever wondered how best to do a quick but long-lasting repair?

LOSS OF A BUTTON

Let's face it, loosing a button or other fastening has to be one of the most common challenges with clothing – they do take a lot of wear and tear, after all. It's well worth having a button pot at home in which you can store all those spare fastenings which are often supplied when buying a new item of clothing; you never know when you might need them! Alternatively, if you have a button that comes loose, add it to the pot and come back to it later.

REATTACHING A BUTTON

1. Take a length of thread from the reel, and cut it approximately 45cm (18in) long. Thread your needle and, taking the two ends of the thread, tie in a knot by creating a loop in the threads, passing the ends through the loop and drawing them tight in a knot at the end.

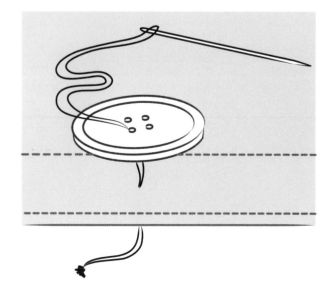

2. Beginning from the back of the fabric, pass the needle up through the fabric, drawing the thread through until the knot is reached. Pass the needle up through one of the holes in the back of the button, again drawing the thread through fully.

3. To help create a stem behind the button, carefully lay a cocktail stick or matchstick on top of the button and pass the needle over the top of this and down through the opposing, or diagonally opposing, hole. Continue down through the fabric close to the initial stitch. Draw the thread through fully; this should hold the stick in place.

Tip: The stem creates a bit of room so that the button doesn't squash the fabric once it is passed through a buttonhole. If you don't need a stem, for example if your button is just for decoration, ignore the cocktail stick part.

4. Repeat another 8 times, alternating between the holes in the button to create an even pattern. On the last time up through the fabric, do not go through the button. Instead slide out the cocktail stick and pass the needle out to the side.

5. Wrap the thread 4 times around the underside of the button to create a bit of a stem and pass the needle through the fabric, close to the previous stitches, to the rear side of the fabric. Staying on the rear side of the fabric, push the needle through the end of a couple of the stitches, creating a loop in the process. Pass the needle through this loop and pull tight to knot; do this twice. Cut the thread close to the knot which you have just created.

Tip: If your button doesn't have holes but instead has a loop on the back, follow the same method as above but just pass the needle through the button loop and back into the fabric. The button itself will create a stem so no need for the cocktail stick either.

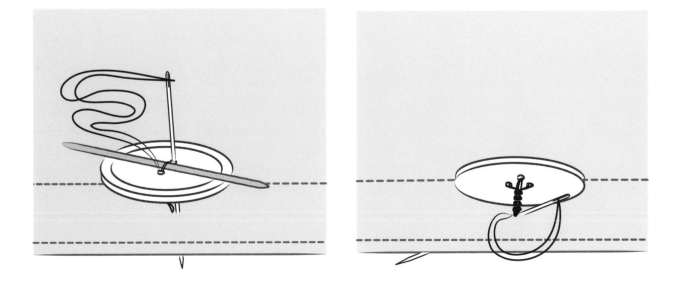

HOOKS AND EYES

Also known as a hook and bar, this is one of the simplest forms of fastening, but very effective and in use a surprising amount in everyday clothing. It can either assist with keeping a closing together while zipping up or to take a little strain off a button. Sometimes the hook can be pulled out of shape, in which case it's best to put a new hook and eye on.

REATTACHING A HOOK AND EYE

1. Where the garment pieces overlap work out the best placement of both hook and eye parts and lightly mark with tailot's chalk or similar.

2. Secure the hook in place by hand stitching on the inner side of the outermost garment part.

3. Follow this by handstitching the eye in place to the outer side of the innermost part of the garment, adjusting its placement if necessary.

PRESS STUDS

Press studs, or poppers as they are sometimes known, can come in a variety of sizes and styles. The hand-sewn variety can easily be fixed with a needle and thread if they come loose, but you might require something stronger and want to replace them with a stronger riveted press stud.

APPLYING A HEAVY-DUTY PRESS STUD

1. Work out your desired placement for the press stud accurately as this is a permanent fixture.

2. Using the cutting die supplied with the kit, press out a hole for the stud parts to go through as marked on both fabric parts.

3. On the innermost garment side marry up the two pieces that make up the male part of the stud, sandwiching the fabric in between. Press together with the tool supplied.

4. Do the same for the female parts on the outermost fabric. Test the stud for correct fastening action.

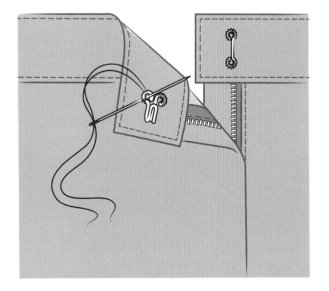

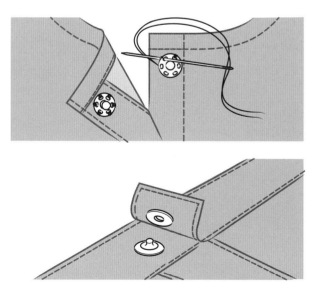

A LOOSE HEMLINE

Everyone will have experienced a fallen hem on a pair of trousers at some point. Although the stitching is designed to withstand plenty of wear and tear, if it becomes damaged at any point then things start to unravel pretty quickly.

MAKING THE REPAIR

On inspection of the hem, firstly determine if you can tie off and secure a part of the fallen hem. If you can, great: this will save you a bit of extra stitching. If you can't, simply remove any loose threads.

1. Begin by lightly pressing the hemline to the wrong side. You should be able to see the original creases. Turn the garment through to the wrong side and pin the hem in place to hold it secure whilst you stitch. Take a needle with a matching thread. Begin by placing a securing stitch on the inner side seam. Do this with a single stitch and tie off in a knot.

2. We're going to use a slipstitch. Carefully slide the needle into the upper folded edge of the hem and guide it along 2cm (³/₄in) inside the hem. Bring it back out of the same folded edge. As the needle comes out pick up just a couple of the main garment threads but stay on the inside of the garment.

3. Pull the needle and thread through fully to the inside so that the thread is through but not too tight or else it will gather the fabric. (You'll see what I mean when you do it.)

4. Re-enter the upper fold just below your picked up thread and slide the needle along another 2cm (³/₄in). Repeat this process all the way around the hemline and tie off back into the side seam.

Tip: If you prefer to use a sewing machine, you largely follow the same approach, but replace the hand stitching with a row of blind-hem stitching.

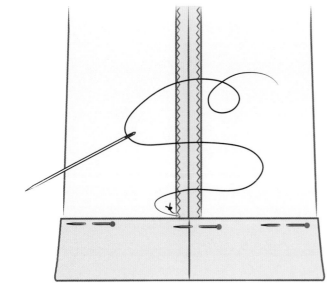

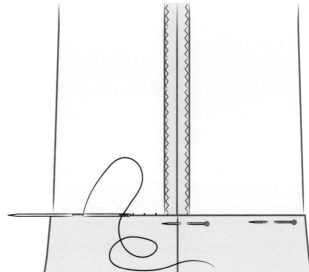

HOLE IN POCKET

This is a common issue for us gents. As we don't have the luxury of carrying a bag, it means our pockets see a lot more action! If you don't repair a hole, think how much it could cost you. You might lose your keys or all that loose change, which could quickly add up, and let's not mention a dropped phone with a cracked screen!

It's often the pocket lining that goes first, which is quick and easy to fix. The solution is largely the same no matter what the garment: a coat, jeans, trousers, etc.

FIXING THE HOLE

If you are repairing a garment where you can access the pocket by turning them through the wrong way, great. If, however, it is inside a lined jacket for instance, you may need to have a search around for a way to get to the inside. On a coat or jacket a good place to look for

an entry point is around the inside of the sleeves, as this is typically the last section of a jacket lining to be sewn. Failing that check the back centre hemline.

1. Okay, now you have access to the pocket lining, you'll find that this is typically joined to a piece of fabric the same as the garment outer. Cut away the stitching where this joins. If not just find a convenient place far enough away from the hole.

2. Cut open any stitches, if there were any used in the original pocket lining. Create a replica pocket lining on paper first by laying the pocket lining out flat and copying around the shape. Don't forget to include a seam allowance of 1.5cm (⅝in).

3. Cut out a replacement pocket from your fabric and stitch as per the original. Neaten edges and trim any excess fabric.

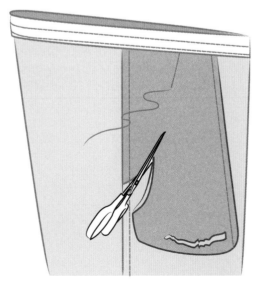

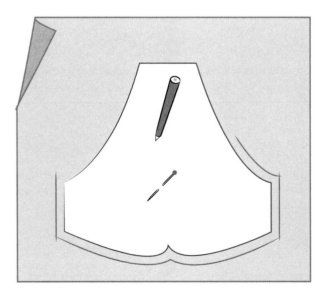

4. Now take the pocket lining and turn it so that the stitching is to the inside. Slip your hand into it and post it into the pocket opening from the inside of the garment. Match the raw edges on both the pocket opening and the pocket lining.

5. Pin the raw edges together, and gently test to ensure correct fit and placement.

6. Now either:
(a) With a needle and thread join the pocket and lining raw edges with a backstitch all the way around, do this with a 5mm (¼in) seam allowance, securing with a knot stitch at the end.
or **(b)** With a sewing machine join the pocket and lining raw edges with an over-edge stitch on a 5mm (¼in) seam allowance. Backstitch at beginning and end. If you find it easier, use the free-arm function (if your machine has it).

7. Remove all pins, if you haven't already done so as you stitched. Turn the pocket through and lightly press. Don't forget to close up any holes in the lining if you needed to gain access to the pocket.

FIND A LOST DRAWSTRING

Losing a drawstring from a garment is annoying but a simple problem to solve, all you need is a trusty safety pin! Let me show you how:

1. Kick things off by removing the whole drawstring from the garment. Simply pull it all the way out.

2. Take your drawstring and pass a safety pin through one end, securing the point as you normally would.

3. Feed the safety pin into one of the openings of the garment, with the drawstring following along behind.

4. Work the safety pin along inside of the waistband channel. Scrunch up the fabric as you go to make this easier.

5. Work the safety pin and drawstring all the way around the waistband and out of the other opening. Now remove the safety pin, and that's it you're all done!

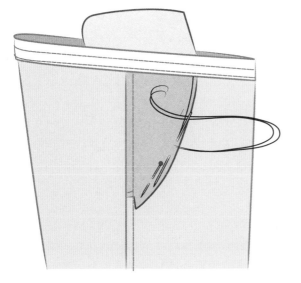

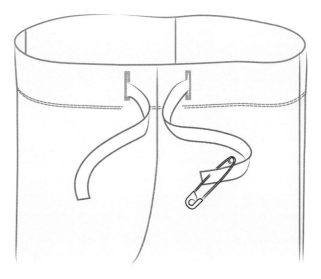

ZIP REPAIRS

Zips are a brilliant invention. When they work we don't think about the wonderful job they do for us. But when there is a problem we can get into a fluster.

The humble zip is made from just a few parts: the slider, the tape and the teeth. The teeth are fixed on either side of the tapes and are interlocked or separated by the slider as it passes over them. Simple yet clever, you can see why the design has hardly changed since the 1850s.

Once a zip is incorporated into a piece of clothing and it goes wrong it can sometimes mean the garment is destined for the back of the drawer, never to be seen again. But with a little time and attention you may be able to salvage it.

I'm going to walk you through three of the most common issues and how to overcome them.

SPLIT ZIP ON AN OPEN-ENDED ZIP

1. Begin by checking the zip slider gap is even and gripping the zip's teeth evenly on both sides, as this could be the reason for the split or loss. Look at the zip slider from the side and squeeze the zip slider back together with pliers if required.

2. You'll notice the zip ends have one thin male part and one square female part. Using pliers remove the top stopper from the side of the zip with the *male* end. Do this by gently working the metal stopper upwards and downwards and from side to side. Don't throw this away, as we'll need it again.

3. Now take the slider to the top of the zip, and remove the male side of the zip from the slider. Take the slider all the way to the bottom of the female side.

4. Replace the stopper at the top of the male side of the zip. Carefully open the gap slightly, either with a small flat screwdriver tip or the back of an old knife. (Do this on a sturdy flat surface like a chopping board and be careful of your fingers.) Once open you can place this back over the zipper tape where you removed it from and secure in place by squeezing together with pliers. Insert the male side and check the zip closes fully.

Zips are great, there's no denying, until they go wrong and then they're known to make a grown man cry. (Yes, I have sobbed over a zip.) But all is not lost – many zips can be salvaged, if not repaired completely.

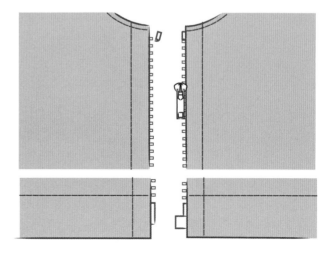

ZIP SLIDER HAS COME OFF THE TOP OF AN OPEN-ENDED ZIP

1. As before, begin by checking the zip slider is gripping the zip's teeth evenly on both sides. Squeeze the zip slider back together with pliers if required.

2. Using your pliers, remove the top stopper from the side of the zip with the *female* end, by gently working the metal stopper upwards and downwards and from side to side. Don't throw this away as we'll need it again.

3. Take the zip slider and, angling it slightly, feed the top teeth of the female side into the opening of the slider. Once in, slide this all the way down to the bottom of the female zip side.

4. Replace the stopper at the top of the female side of the zip. Do this by carefully opening the gap slightly, either with a fine flat screwdriver tip or the back of an old knife. (Do this on a sturdy flat surface like a chopping board and be careful of your fingers.) Once opened up you can place this back over the zipper tape where you removed it from and secure in place by squeezing together with pliers. With the slider at the bottom of the zip, insert the male side and check the zip closes fully.

MISSING TEETH IN A CLOSED-END ZIP

Typically when you have missing zip teeth your zip's days are numbered. However, if the gap is low down enough you may be able to salvage it, though you will shorten it in the process. Ideally the slider is still on both sides of the zip and below the missing teeth – if so skip to step 2.

1. If the slider is off one side of the tape move it until it is just above the point of the zip where the teeth are missing. Give the slider a little wiggle to get it onto both sides of the zipper tape. Use downward pressure to help take it past the gap.

2. Holding the zipper tape flat and all teeth touching together, very gently slide the slider up past the gap.

3. With a needle and thread create a new bottom stopper by stitching across the closed zipper tape, just above the missing teeth. (You can use a sewing machine to do this: make sure you have the feet dogs down, and use a wide zigzag stitch.) Secure the thread with a knot and trim away ends.

4. Carefully test the zip out to ensure it stops at your newly sewn bottom stopper.

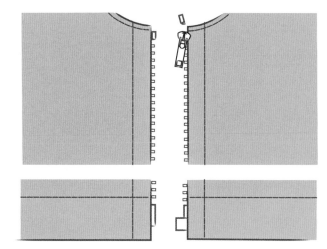

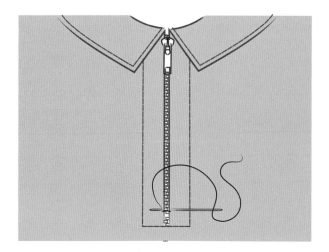

REPAIRING TORN FABRIC

Another tear you may have experienced is when you've torn the fabric of your favourite top or trousers. Do not panic, as there maybe a way to save them from the bin!

If the tear is on a section of medium- to heavy-weight fabric you could get away with using an iron-on fusible backing.

1. Trim back any wispy fibres from the tear. From the wrong side align the torn edges as best you can.

2. Cut a piece of fusible backing to be approximately 2cm (¾in) larger on all sides of the tear.

3. Turn the garment inside out and place the fusible backing (shiny adhesive side down) on top of the tear.

4. Check the manufacturer's advice for your iron heat setting and press the top of the fusible backing. Do not use steam or move the iron, just apply downward pressure for the duration recommended on the manufacturer's guidelines. It really is as easy as that.

Alternatively, on a light-weight fabric such as cotton or viscose, the tear can be repaired by neatly stitching the tear back together.

1. Carefully remove any little loose fibres from the tear to give a neat edge.

2. Working from the wrong side of the fabric, take a threaded needle with a matching thread and place a securing stitch just outside of the tear at one end. Do this as just a single stitch tied off in a knot.

3. Using small, closely placed stitches, stitch along the tear just a few fabric threads at a time. Picking up a couple of threads from each side of the tear. Gently draw together the raw edges as you bring the needle and thread through fully.

4. Continue along the tear until you reach the other end. Put a securing stitch in place and trim away any excess threads. Finish with a light press from both sides.

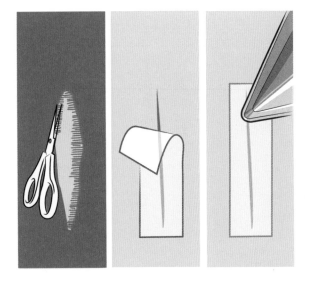

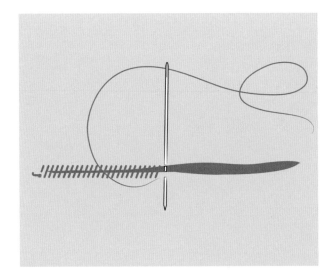

REPAIR A TORN SEAM

There are two ways that a seam tends to tear: along the stitching or along the fabric. If the seam has torn follow the steps below. If the fabric is torn follow the instructions opposite for Repairing torn fabric.

1. Locate the tear and secure or remove any trailing loose threads. Carefully pin along the desired seam to rejoin the fabric parts. With a threaded and knotted needle place a securing stitch in the seam allowance 1.5cm (⅝in) before the seam opening. This is just a single stitch that is tied off in a knot.

2. We are now going to backstitch along the seam. This will give the seam line strength and should reduce the chances of it tearing again. Do this by slowly stitching along the original stitch line by moving along 3–4mm (⅛in) and going through both fabric layers, then move backwards half of the distance and come back through the fabric layers to your starting side.

3. Backstitch all the way along the torn seam, coming in slightly if the fabric itself is torn. At the end of the gap rejoin the original seam and continue past it 1.5cm (⅝in). Tie off and trim the thread ends.

HOW TO CLOSE A SEAM ON A TIE

A fairly common problem for us chaps, although probably found more on school ties which see a lot of action in the playground! It's always best to try and catch this early to prevent the whole tie opening up.

1. First things first, you need to stop it getting any worse. Thread a needle and place a catch stitch just above the point where the seam has opened. Tie this off.

2. Lay the tie on a flat surface and align the original seam. You can pin in place but to be honest that sometimes makes it a bit trickier. Slip your needle through just one layer where the seams join and slide it along approximately 1.5cm (⅝in), bringing it back out on the same seam line (slip stitch). Draw the thread all the way through. Where your needle comes out slip it into the opposite seam and slide it along a further 1.5cm (⅝in).

3. Continue this method along the seam, alternating every 1.5cm (⅝in) from one seam to the other. As you bring the needle out for the last time, make a final few catch stitches and tie off the thread ends. Ties should have a certain bounce to them so there is no need to press.

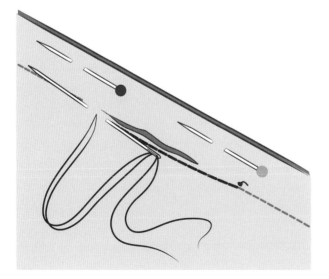

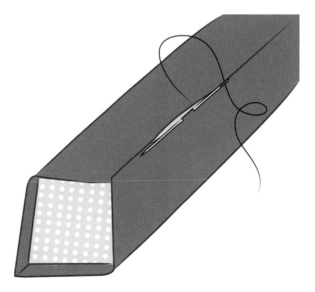

MAKE IT LIVE LONGER

It's official, clothes should last longer than one season! Different fabrics require different treatment, but with a little care your clothes can last for many years and still look like new.

Maintaining your clothes

WASH YOUR CLOTHES ONLY WHEN DIRTY

This might sound obvious, but with the convenience of the washer/dryer and the urge to always make up a complete load, we tend to over wash our clothes. But every time they are washed the fabric fibres will weaken and the colour will fade. So rather than washing clothes after just a few hours of wear, try hanging them up ready for the next outing.

Not only will you reduce your washing and ironing but you are doing your bit for the environment, too!

INVEST IN A LINT ROLLER

When I say invest, it's not as if a lint roller will break the bank or anything – you can buy one quite cheaply – but it's sure to keep your clothes looking their best, be it a humble pair of black trousers or a thick winter coat. In the process of lint rolling your clothes you'll also reduce the need to wash those items so frequently, too.

KNOW YOUR REDS FROM YOUR BLUES

Separate your colours! When working through your washing pile, think through the colours which run and fade more easily, i.e. your reds and blues. We all have the tendency to wash anything with colour together, especially when there is a growing wash basket to battle through, but bear in mind a yellow dress and a red T-shirt hastily thrust in the machine together could make for a costly combination.

TURN YOUR DENIM INSIDE-OUT

Fabric such as denim can contain a lot of dye when it is constructed. By turning the garment inside-out for washing it will greatly reduce the heavily dyed surface coming in direct contract with other fabrics. Wash denim separately for the first couple of washes as the dye is most likely to run then.

CLOSE ZIPS, VELCRO AND CLASPS

Just take a moment to think of the different fabrics and fastenings which we bundle into a single wash. To make sure the more delicate fabrics such as polyesters, satins and lace trims last longer, I recommend that you close any hard and abrasive fastenings like zips, Velcro and hook and eyes before washing so they are less likely to snag.

REDUCE THE TUMBLE-DRIED CREASE

Tumble drying is a great quick fix but that benefit can be undone if you don't remove the clothes quickly after the cycle has finished. If you leave clothing, particularly cottons, sitting in a warm dyer they will develop very deep creases, causing you a bigger headache when you come to iron them. Hang or fold the load as soon as possible.

FOLD OR HANG?

Space can be an issue in most households, so if, like me, you don't have the luxury of a walk-in wardrobe you need to prioritize your hanging space. All the items that don't fold well, like jackets, blazers, tailored trousers, dresses and shirts, should get priority, then any space you have remaining should go to light-weight tops. Where possible use a tubular hanger rather than a wire hanger, this will help maintain the natural shape of the garment. Jumpers can stretch on a hanger, especially heavy knits, so it's best to fold them and store them in a drawer.

DON'T HANG ABOUT WITH STAINS

Accidents happen and clothes will get marked. To stand the best possible chance of removing the mark you must act quickly. Don't leave it to the next time you happen to put a load of washing on. Remove the garment and with warm water, a clean cloth and a small amount of washing power gently sponge out the affected area. If need be soak the item with a dash of stain removal liquid before washing.

A PRESSING MATTER

My time in the army taught me a good deal about ironing and the damage it can do if you aren't careful. I don't mean the comedy sketch staple of an iron-shaped hole in a shirt! It's more the fact that if you choose the wrong heat setting you can damage the fibres beyond repair. Also, if you repeatedly iron the same areas of a garment, for example, the crease on a pair of trousers, you'll end up with shiny patches.

Read the manufacturer's guidance, and if in doubt use a plain pillow case on top of delicate fabrics then iron onto that in order to protect them.

READ THE WASHING LABELS – TWICE!

Read first when buying a new item of clothing
If you know you don't ever get round to dry cleaning or hand washing should you buy it in the first place?

Read second when washing for the first time
The symbols and guidance has been written for a reason (see page 170 for a run down). I'd say accept the advice and let your clothes look better for longer!

LAUNDRY SYMBOLS EXPLAINED

The best way to keep your clothes in top condition is to pay attention to the advice on the label.

MACHINE-WASHING SYMBOLS: We all have a favourite wash cycle we use for most of our washing loads, but it is worth following the recommended washing cycle for individual garments if you want clothes to last.

- ⊔ The basic symbol which shows that a garment can be machine washed
- ⊔ If a number is present this represents the maximum water temperature
- ⊔ An addition of a line below the basic symbol is suggesting choosing a synthetic cycle.
- ⊔ If a dashed line is present, this suggests choosing a delicate wash cycle.
- ⊠ Do NOT machine wash! This symbol is likely to be paired with a dry-cleaning symbol.

HAND-WASHING SYMBOLS: I'm not sure which I dislike more, the hand-wash symbol or the dry-clean symbol. Either one requires that little more effort and or expense. But what's the alternative – putting a hand-wash only garment in the machine only to be disappointed that it has shrunk?

- ⊍ Hand wash in warm water.

WASHING SYMBOLS FOR BLEACH: You may love or loathe bleach but be sure to check the label before using. Here are the symbols to look out for:
- △ You can use bleach during the washing process
- ⊠ Do NOT use bleach

DRYING SYMBOLS: As with washing, before you tumble dry something for the first time check the label for the suggested setting. It could mean the difference between being able to wear your garment again or passing it to the kids for their teddy bears!

- ▢ The basic symbol which indicates an item can be tumble dried
- ▣ If the basic symbol has an additional dot, choose a low heat setting
- ▣ The addition of two dots recommends a medium heat setting
- ⊠ Do NOT tumble dry!
- ▥ Drip drying on a clothes rack is recommended for these garments
- ▢ Line drying or hanging is recommended for these garments
- ▭ To dry, lay the item flat to maintain the shape

DRY-CLEANING: Dry-cleaning is a process which uses chemicals to clean clothes. Manufacturers often recommend dry-cleaning when a delicate material or trim is used on a garment which won't withstand the rough and tumble of a washing machine or tumble dryer. When buying clothes look out for the circular symbol. If the circle contains a letter this is specific chemical information for the cleaning company.

- ○ Suitable for dry-cleaning, the basic symbol
- ⊗ Do NOT dry-clean, as the chemicals used may damage the fabric

IRONING: The number of dots in the iron symbol recommend how hot the iron should be to prevent damaging the fabric.

- ⊿ Cool iron, with a temperature up to 110°C – perfect for acrylics, acetates and nylons
- ⊿ Warm iron, with a temperature up to 150°C – perfect for polyester mixes and woollens
- ⊿ Hot iron, with a temperature up to 200°C – perfect for linens and cottons
- ⊠ Do NOT iron anything with this symbol as it is likely to cause damage to the fabric

A little bit of polish

I couldn't resist adding this section. I'm a stickler for polished shoes! I think you can tell a lot about someone from their shoes and how well they are looked after. If you've gone to all the effort of making or altering a garment to create the perfect fit, and ironing your outfit for a neat finish, the last thing you want to complete your well-turned-out look is a pair of dull, dirty shoes!

If you are investing in good pair of shoes then a little TLC every so often will help them last a lifetime, or at least decades.

Don't get me wrong, we're not talking about boots fit for the parade square that you can see your face in, but you should look to polish your worn shoes on a weekly basis, or of course when marked or dirty.

Another tip is to let the shoes breathe. The best way to do this is not to wear the same pair two days running; try to alternate between at least a couple of pairs to prolong their condition.

If your shoes get soaking wet, please don't shove them on a radiator or in front of the fire – the leather will crack and perish. Instead, stuff them with scrunched-up newspaper and place them in a warm (not hot), dry room and allow them to dry naturally. Change the paper regularly to draw all the moisture out of the leather.

I recommend having a separate set of cloths and brushes for each colour polish you use.

MINI SHOE-SHINE KIT

Cream Polish – polish is used to clean and condition the leather. You can buff the polish to create a limited shine. As a minimum, have a tin of brown and a tin of black polish in your kit.

Wax – wax is optional, but it's like a top coat. It protects the polished leather and you can also buff it to create a high-gloss shine.

Cloths – you need two cloths, one for applying the polish and the second for the final buff and shine.

Brushes – use a larger brush with soft bristles for buffing and a smaller brush to apply the wax.

HOW TO POLISH SHOES

1. Before you can polish you need to start with a clean pair of shoes, using the larger brush to remove any surface dirt.

2. Apply a small amount of the cream polish to a cloth (matching the polish colour with the shoes) and rub over the shoes. If you have any worn areas, say on the toe or heel, pay extra attention to these areas when applying the polish.
   Tip: Less is more! You only need a small amount of polish; if you use too much it will build up over time and crack.

3. Taking the larger brush, rub the brush all over the surface of the shoe until you have created a light shine. Don't be shy, get stuck in!

4. Using the small brush, apply a thin layer of wax all over the shoes, and rub in to the leather.

5. With the second cloth set to work on the final buff and shine. Continue until you have your desired gloss effect.

Glossary

BASTING: A temporary long-length stitch used to hold sections of a garment together before stitching. Helpful for pleats.

BIAS: The diagonal direction of a piece of fabric, running at 45° to the selvedge. A fabric cut on the bias has more stretch to it.

CASING: A channel sewn into a section of material for something to be inserted into it, such as drawstring on a waistband.

CLIPPING/TRIMMING: Corners and curves both inward and outward need to be released to look their very best. Cut close to but not through your stitch line.

CUTTING LINE: Multi-size patterns have various cut lines. These vary from a solid line through to a dotted line and all variables in between. Note your one and stick to it when cutting out.

EASING/GATHERING: Shown on a pattern as a row of two dashed lines depicting where you should place two rows of loose stitches to draw the fabric gently together.

FACING: A section of fabric sewn and turned to the inside of a garment, such as necklines, armholes and waistlines, to give more structure, a neater finish and increase comfort.

FEED DOGS: These are the gnarled teeth of your sewing machine that help to move your fabric through as you stitch. The mechanism inside controls the speed and distance they travel.

FOLD/FOLD LINE: If a piece is symmetrical you may be able to cut this out on a folded part of fabric. Shown as a double-pointed bar with two 90° angles.

GRAIN: Shown as double-pointed arrows, this is the natural direction in which the fabric is constructed, also known as the warp. (The weft is the direction from selvedge to selvedge.)

INTERFACING: Some garments and fabric require stabilizing to look their best. This is normally shown on the paper pattern as a light patchy effect. Can be either sewn in or ironed on.

LAYERING/GRADING: To reduce the weight of bulky seams you can trim back the seam allowance of one or more layers. Cut at different distances to the stitch line to allow the seam to sit flat.

LENGTHENING OR SHORTENING LINES: These are represented on a pattern as two straight lines. Either cut your paper pattern here to extend or fold a pleat to shorten as desired.

NAP: Some fabrics when constructed have a preferred direction that the fibres lay in: this is called the nap. Brush your hand gently over the right side and feel for the smoother texture.

NEATENING/EDGE FINISH: The process of stopping raw edges from fraying. Do this by either zigzag stitching within the seam allowance or by over-edge stitching the raw edge. Other options include pinking shears and overlockers.

NOTCHES: These combinations of triangles can be seen as singles, doubles, triples, both hollow and solid. They are there to help you match pattern pieces when you are constructing. Match notches equally, for example a single to a single. etc.

RIGHT SIDE: You can tell the right side of a fabric by looking closely and spotting the side that has a better quality finish or a stronger and clearer pattern.

SEAM ALLOWANCE: This is the distance from the cut raw edge to the stitch line.

SELVEDGE: The raw edges of the fabric from manufacturing construction. They tend to be approximately 1.5cm (5/8in) wide and run the full length of the fabric.

STAY STITCH: Finer fabrics have a tendency to be pulled out of shape during a make. Avoid this is by stay stitching: placing a row of stitches within your seam allowance.

TAILOR TACKS: The traditional method to mark out points, these are made with a threaded needle being passed through the pattern and fabric then cut off to leave a long thread end.

WRONG SIDE: This will be the less finished side of your fabric. Look for less of a distinctive pattern and less smooth finish.

YOKE: Typically found on a shirt, this is the upper shoulder section. Normally constructed as two parts that join the front and back panels along with the collar and arms. The top of a skirt can also be referred to as a yoke.

Resources

It's great to create a store of the basic materials and tools but when you undertake a new project it often starts with a visit to a local haberdashery or placing an order online (always order a sample first to ensure it's what you wanted). Here are a few resources which we turned to during the making of this book. Most of them will get you up and running from the comfort of your home.

UNITED KINGDOM

GIRL CHARLEE
The Jersey and knits specialist
www.girlcharlee.co.uk
www.girlcharlee.com

ETERNAL MAKER
Fantastic range of cottons and organic fabrics
www.eternalmaker.com

PLUSH ADDICT
Huge range of fabric and haberdashery resources
www.plushaddict.co.uk

FABRIC GOD MOTHER
Wide range of on-trend fabrics plus all the trimmings
www.fabricgodmother.co.uk

GUTHRIE AND GHANI
Owned and run by 2013 Sewing Bee Finalist Lauren Guthrie, they stock loads of gorgeous fabrics
www.guthrie-ghani.co.uk

FRINGE
A bright an airy shop stocking fabulous fabrics, wonderful wools and loads of cool tools. They even run sewing classes on site.
www.fringe108.london

FASHION FABRICS
More fabric than you can shake a stick at. Massive stock at really reasonable prices
www.fashionfabricsbath.co.uk

JOHN LEWIS
www.johnlewis.com

LIBERTY
www.liberty.co.uk

THE FOLD LINE
Research patterns and read reviews from other like-minded stitchers
www.thefoldline.com

COLETTE
Lovely modern patterns with an active blog
www.colettepatterns.com

JUST BETWEEN FRIENDS
Quilting and cotton fabric stockists
www.justbetweenfriends.co.uk

UNITED STATES

FABRIC.COM
Huge range of fabrics available online, ranging from heavy denim to light silk
www.fabric.com

FASHION FABRICS CLUB
If you want choice & variety then take a look at Fashion Fabrics Club: their huge stock offers up pages of different prints in every possible fabric
www.fashionfabricsclub.com

FABRIC WORM
Fantastic range of cottons with a great choice of organic fabrics
www.fabricworm.com

MOOD FABRICS
From fabric to buttons to trim finishes you will find something you like on Mood Fabrics
www.moodfabrics.com

THE FABRIC STORE
Beautiful and refined selection of fabrics including high-quality New Zealand Merion wool jerseys that they ship around the globe
www.thefabricstoreusa.com
shop.thefabricstore.co.nz

OLIVER+ S
Wide range of patterns especially for children and another great blog
http://oliverands.com

AUSTRALIA

THE REMNANT WAREHOUSE
Huge range of fabrics, lace, trims plus the essential haberdashery stock, all at great prices.
www.theremnantwarehouse.com.au

KELANI FABRIC
Wide on-trend & seasonal fabrics including a wide choice of Australian designers
www.kelanifabric.com.au

LINCRAFT
Great range of haberdashery resources with a range of fabrics by the meter. Lincraft have a series of stores around Australia & New Zealand.
www.lincraft.com.au

THE FABRIC CLOSET
Fantastic range of cottons and organic fabrics
www.thefabriccloset.com.au

If you want to find something a little more unusual or support small producers I would recommend having a browse on *www.etsy.com*

BLOGS
Blogs are a great way to find inspiration, advice and feel part of a community. You can follow my progress and projects on my blog *www.sewwhatsnew.co.uk*

Index

Acknowledgements

Books are rarely written by one person alone, and *Make it, Own it, Love it* is no different. It has most definitely been a team effort. I'd like to take this opportunity to send out a huge heartfelt thanks to the following people:

To the whole team at Jacqui Small LLP. You are an absolute joy to work with and I feel honoured to be a part of the family, but especially:

– the wonderful Jacqui Small for seeing in me a book just waiting to be written.

– Sian Parkhouse and Ezster Karpati, whose direction and knowledge kept us delivering even in the tightest of time constraints.

– creative genius Rachel Cross, who brought this book to life with elegance and beauty. Teamed with our fantastic photographer Simon Brown, your eye for just the right shot was invaluable

– Simon's expert assistants Astrid Templier and Milo Brown; you're both amazingly talented and it was a real pleasure to work with you. Astrid gets a special mention for also modelling at short notice.

– the excellent detailed work of our illustrators Kate Simunek and Serena Olivier.

The whole marketing team who will hand deliver every book (you do do that, right?)

Finally the team of models who have made each garment shine, with special thanks to Sian Lewis – who would have thought an internship would have included a spot of modelling too!

We had a few lovely locations that not only agreed to let us in to disrupt their day but actually welcomed us. So a big thank you goes out to Jane Cumberbatch and her beautiful house, Judith and Julie at Fringe in Muswell Hill, and all the team at Drink, Shop and Do.

A special thanks has to go out to my family. Max and Evie have had many days where I've been busy and couldn't come and play. While we believe it's healthy for them to see us working hard to achieve something, it's also good to have a balance, so I look forward to addressing that.

Without a doubt I'm saving my biggest thank you for my loving wife and best friend Gemma. You have endured many long nights not only discussing sewing, but also in helping me writing this book, whether it be as research, sourcing materials, generating ideas or proofreading. You are truly amazing and I feel forever blessed to have you by my side. You rock!

And, of course, thanks to all of you lovely stitchers out there who are reading this book, watched the show or take time from your days to chat to me in the street. You never fail to brighten my day and make my belief ring true that the sewing and craft community really is full of fantastic people.